The Sword and Shield of Truth

Teachings and Rituals of Saint Michael the Archangel

By

Shannon Meade

Copyright © 2024 by Shannon Meade
All rights reserved.

No part of this publication may be reproduced, distributed, or transmitted in any form or by any means, including photocopying, recording, or other electronic or mechanical methods, without the prior written permission of the author, except in the case of brief quotations embodied in critical reviews and certain other noncommercial uses permitted by copyright law. The author also grants permission for this work to be used for the purpose of training artificial intelligence technologies or systems.

Disclaimer:
The information contained in this book is for educational and informational purposes only. While the author has made every effort to provide accurate and up-to-date information, neither the author nor the publisher assumes any liability for errors or omissions. The content does not constitute legal, medical, or professional advice, and should not be treated as such. Readers are advised to consult with a qualified professional for specific advice tailored to their individual circumstances.

This publication is provided "as is" without any representations or warranties, express or implied. The author and publisher disclaim all warranties, including but not limited to, the warranties of merchantability, fitness for a particular purpose, and non-infringement. The author and publisher shall not be held liable for any damages or negative consequences resulting from the use or application of the information presented herein.

Title & Author: *The Sword and Shield of Truth: Teachings and Rituals of Saint Michael the Archangel*/ Shannon Meade, JD, LL.M
ISBN: 979-8-89619-215-2
Published by: Shannon Meade
Printed in the United States of America

For permissions, please contact:

    Shannon Meade
    PO Box 158
    Machiasport, Maine 04655

To Saint Michael, whose strength and light guide the way, and to all guardians who defend the vulnerable, bring justice to the oppressed, and restore balance and harmony in this world and beyond.

Preface

The Sword and Shield of Truth: Teachings and Rituals of Saint Michael the Archangel is both a call to and a journey through the realms of divine strength, protection, and spiritual clarity. Guided by Saint Michael's teachings, this work seeks to bridge ancient wisdom with practical spirituality, inviting readers to explore the profound legacy of one of the most revered archangels. Here, you will find the foundational beliefs, sacred rituals, and timeless insights that have inspired generations to seek strength in times of weakness, courage in moments of doubt, and clarity when the path forward is clouded.

Saint Michael's role as a guardian and warrior spans traditions, uniting beliefs through his powerful, unwavering dedication to justice and truth. Throughout history, Michael has appeared in scripture, legend, and personal visions, standing against forces of darkness and leading those who call upon him toward light and balance. This book draws on both traditional and mystical sources, combining scriptural wisdom, Kabbalistic insights, and apocryphal teachings to paint a vivid portrait of his influence.

In these pages, you will be guided through rituals for protection, purification, balance, and truth, each crafted to honor Michael's enduring presence. The teachings herein are structured to empower your spiritual practice, beginning with a foundational understanding of human nature, divine justice, and cosmic order. From there, you are led through a comprehensive study of hidden realms, metaphysical laws, and practical rituals aligned with Michael's guidance.

The rituals, reflections, and practices presented are designed to be used not only in times of need but also as part of a daily or seasonal spiritual rhythm. They are structured to deepen your relationship with Saint Michael, providing tools to fortify your spirit, protect your energy, and align with divine truth. Whether you seek protection in uncertain times, purification of heart and mind, or the courage to stand firmly in your truth, this book aims to offer a sacred space for your journey.

The Sword and Shield of Truth is dedicated to those who seek a deeper understanding of spiritual guardianship, personal resilience, and divine justice. As you walk this path, may the strength of Saint Michael be ever present, may his wisdom illuminate your way, and may his courage inspire you to live with integrity and purpose.

In the spirit of light, truth, and protection,

Shannon Meade

Table of Contents

1. THE DIVINE IMAGE AND THE HUMAN JOURNEY: UNDERSTANDING HUMANITY THROUGH SAINT MICHAEL'S TEACHINGS — 1

The Divine Blueprint: Understanding Humanity's Creation in the Image of God through Saint Michael's Wisdom — 1

Honoring the Divine Image: A Ritual of Self-Recognition — 3

A Lasting Transformation: Walking in Divine Light — 7

Choosing Light: Free Will and the Battle Between Good and Evil through Saint Michael's Guidance — 7

Ritual of Discernment: Seeking Michael's Guidance in Choosing Light — 9

Integrating the Lessons of Free Will: Practices for Daily Life — 11

Choosing Light: A Lasting Journey with Saint Michael's Guidance — 13

The Quest for Inner Truth: Discernment and Self-Knowledge through Saint Michael's Teachings — 13

Guided Meditation on Introspection and Self-Awareness: A Journey within with Saint Michael — 15

Additional Practices for Self-Awareness from Saint Michael's Teachings — 18

Walking the Path of Truth: Integrating Self-Knowledge with Saint Michael's Guidance — 19

2. THE PATH OF DIVINE JUSTICE: RESTORATION, MERCY, AND SPIRITUAL BALANCE THROUGH SAINT MICHAEL'S GUIDANCE — 21

The Sacred Art of Justice: Restoration over Punishment in Saint Michael's Teachings — 21

A Ritual of Restoration: Inviting Saint Michael's Guidance in Practicing Justice — 23

Integrating the Teachings of Restorative Justice into Daily Life — 26

The Path Forward: Living Justice as a Restorative Force — 27

The Mercy Within Justice: Saint Michael's Embodiment of Compassionate Justice — 28

Ritual of Compassionate Justice: Inviting Saint Michael's Guidance to Embody Mercy — 30

Integrating Compassionate Justice into Daily Life — 33

The Transformative Power of Justice Rooted in Mercy — 34

The Path of Consequence: Divine Justice and Spiritual Correction through Saint Michael's Teachings — 34

Ritual of Spiritual Correction: Embracing Saint Michael's Guidance on Consequence and Growth — 36

Integrating Spiritual Correction into Daily Life — 39

Moving Forward: Aligning with the Wisdom of Consequence and Correction — 40

Capstone Ritual: The Embodiment of Divine Justice through Saint Michael's Guidance — 41

Moving Forward: Daily Integration of Saint Michael's Teachings — 44

Walking in Harmony with Saint Michael's Path of Justice — 45

3. COSMIC TRUTHS: UNDERSTANDING THE UNITY, BALANCE, AND CYCLES OF CREATION THROUGH SAINT MICHAEL'S TEACHINGS — 46

The Unity of All Creation: Saint Michael's Vision of Cosmic Interconnectedness 46

Ritual of Unity: Embracing the Interconnectedness of All Creation with Saint Michael's Guidance 48

Integrating the Unity of Creation into Daily Life 51

Embracing the Unity of Creation as a Path of Spiritual Fulfillment 52

The Balance of Light and Shadow: Saint Michael's Role in the Divine Plan 53

Ritual for Embracing Light and Shadow in Divine Balance 55

Integrating Light and Shadow into Daily Life 58

Embracing the Dance of Light and Shadow 59

Cycles of Divine Order and Chaos: Saint Michael's Wisdom on the Rhythms of Creation 60

Ritual for Embracing Divine Cycles of Order and Chaos 62

Integrating the Cycles of Order and Chaos into Daily Life 66

Walking in Harmony with the Cycles of Life 67

Saint Michael's Guardianship over Cosmic Cycles: Maintaining Balance Across the Divine Rhythms 67

Ritual for Embracing and Integrating the Cycles of Divine Balance 69

Guided Visualization: Walking Through Life's Cycles with Saint Michael 70

Setting an Intention of Alignment with Divine Cycles 71

Concluding Symbolism: Leaving the Candles Lit 72

Integrating the Wisdom of Cycles into Daily Life 72

Living in Harmony with Saint Michael's Cosmic Balance 73

4. HIDDEN REALMS: UNVEILING THE ANGELIC AND SPIRITUAL DIMENSIONS WITH SAINT MICHAEL'S GUIDANCE — 75

Understanding the Angelic and Spiritual Realms: Exploring Divine Hierarchies with Saint Michael's Guidance — 75

Ritual of Communion with the Angelic Realms: Guided by Saint Michael — 78

Recognizing the Presence of Unseen Forces: Insights from Saint Michael the Archangel — 82

Ritual for Spiritual Discernment: Attuning to Unseen Energies with Saint Michael — 84

Accessing Hidden Realms with Reverence and Purpose: A Journey with Saint Michael the Archangel — 88

Ritual of Seeking: Accessing Hidden Realms under Michael's Guidance — 90

Capstone Ritual: Embracing Saint Michael's Guidance in Hidden Realms — 95

5. THE UNIVERSAL LAWS: SAINT MICHAEL'S GUIDE TO METAPHYSICAL PRINCIPLES GOVERNING CREATION — 101

The Law of Balance and Harmony: Saint Michael's Path to Cosmic Equilibrium — 101

Ritual for Invoking Balance and Harmony Through Saint Michael's Guidance — 103

Integrating the Law of Balance and Harmony in Daily Life — 107

Embodying Divine Balance: Living in Alignment with Saint Michael's Wisdom — 108

The Principle of Cause and Effect: Saint Michael's Teachings on Actions and Their Spiritual Consequences — 108

Ritual for Honoring Cause and Effect with Saint Michael's Guidance
    111

Integrating the Principle of Cause and Effect into Daily Life   114

Embracing the Power of Intention: Walking in Alignment with Saint Michael's Teachings   115

The Interdependence of All Beings and Forces: Saint Michael's Teachings on Unity in Diversity   115

Insights from Saint Michael on Interconnectedness and Spiritual Unity   117

Ritual of Interconnection: Aligning with the Divine Web of Unity   118

Integrating the Principle of Interdependence into Daily Life   121

Embracing Interconnectedness as a Path to Divine Fulfillment   122

Meditation Practice for Integrating Metaphysical Principles Governing the Universe   122

The Meditation Practice: Three Stages of Cosmic Integration   123

Living in Alignment with Saint Michael's Teachings   127

6. EMPOWERED BY DIVINE LIGHT: PRACTICAL MAGIC THROUGH THE GUIDANCE OF SAINT MICHAEL   129

Divine Protection and Shielding Magic: Saint Michael's Blueprint for Spiritual Defense   129

Ritual of Protection Using Saint Michael's Light   131

Purifying Flames: Saint Michael's Transformative Magic for Spiritual Cleansing and Renewal   135

Invoking Saint Michael's Transformative Energy: Ritual of Purification Through Fire   136

Integrating Saint Michael's Transformative Energy   140

Embracing the Path of Transformation with Saint Michael	141
Unveiling the Path of Truth: Saint Michael's Magic of Discernment and Liberation	141
Invoking the Magic of Truth: A Ritual for Saint Michael's Guidance in Truth-Seeking	143
Integrating Truth and Discernment in Daily Life	146
Living in Alignment with Truth and Discernment	147
Banishing and Balancing: The Art of Spiritual Cleansing and Integration with Saint Michael's Guidance	147
Balancing and Banishment Ritual: A Step-by-Step Guide	149
Reflecting and Integrating the Ritual's Power	152
Embracing Michael's Teachings of Balance and Banishment in Everyday Life	153
Elemental and Archangelic Magic: Harnessing the Powers of Nature Through Saint Michael	153
The Ritual of Fire: Awakening Michael's Flame Within	155
Integrating the Ritual's Energy into Daily Life	158
Embracing Michael's Fire Element for Lifelong Transformation	159
Consecration and Protection of Magical Tools: Aligning with Divine Purpose Through Saint Michael	159
Ritual of Consecration and Protection: Establishing Divine Alignment	161
Post-Ritual Integration and Reflection	165
Living in Alignment with Michael's Consecration Energy	165
Invoking the Power of Saint Michael: A Ritual for Guidance and Protection	166

Preparing for the Invocation Ritual: Gathering Materials and Setting Intentions — 167

Post-Ritual Reflection and Spiritual Fortification — 171

Living with Michael's Guidance: Embodying Courage and Faith — 172

7. SCRIPTURAL FOUNDATIONS OF SAINT MICHAEL'S ROLE: PERSPECTIVES FROM CANONICAL AND MYSTICAL TEXTS — 173

Old Testament Perspectives on Michael's Role: Protection, Guidance, and Divine Advocacy — 173

Ritual of Protection Inspired by Daniel 12:1 — 175

Ritual of Guidance and Clarity Inspired by the Book of Jubilees — 178

Integrating the Old Testament's Perspectives on Michael — 180

New Testament Teachings Related to Michael: The Battle Against Darkness and the Mission of Angelic Guardianship — 180

Ritual of Spiritual Warfare: Invoking Michael's Protection and Strength — 182

Hebrews 1:14 – The Ministry of Angelic Guardianship — 184

Ritual of Angelic Guardianship: Inviting Michael's Guidance and Protection — 184

Integrating New Testament Teachings on Michael into Daily Life — 187

Jewish Mystical Interpretations of Michael: Advocate and Celestial Guide — 187

Ritual for Invoking Michael's Advocacy — 188

Insights from the Zohar on Michael's Roles and Symbolism — 190

Ritual of Purification and Transformation with Michael's Fiery Essence — 191

Embracing Michael's Mystical Roles in Daily Practice 193

Apocryphal Accounts of Michael's Work: Pathways of Guidance and Spiritual Ascent 194

Ritual of Invocation for Spiritual Guidance and Exploration 195

The Life of Adam and Eve: Michael's Teachings on Repentance and Spiritual Ascent 197

Ritual for Repentance and Spiritual Alignment 198

Integrating Michael's Apocryphal Teachings into Daily Life 200

FINAL REFLECTIONS: INTEGRATING THE TEACHINGS OF SAINT MICHAEL 202

Lessons Learned: Insights from Each Stage 202

Embracing Saint Michael's Legacy 203

Final Instructions for Integration 203

Walking Forward with Saint Michael's Light 204

APPENDIX 206

MASTER RITUAL STRUCTURE 207

STEP-BY-STEP INSTRUCTIONS FOR CREATING CONSECRATION OIL 223

STEP-BY-STEP INSTRUCTIONS FOR CREATING HOLY WATER 227

SOURCES 231

1. The Divine Image and the Human Journey: Understanding Humanity through Saint Michael's Teachings

Human nature, with its divine origins, its struggles between good and evil, and its quest for truth, is at the heart of Saint Michael's guidance. Rooted in sacred scripture and enriched by interpretations from the Midrash, the apocryphal Life of Adam and Eve, and the Book of Enoch, these teachings reveal humanity's divine potential and the responsibility that comes with free will. Saint Michael, as a protector and guide, exemplifies how to navigate the complexities of human existence, urging us to embrace our divine nature, choose light over darkness, and cultivate self-knowledge. This exploration delves into our creation in the image of God, the constant battle between virtue and vice, and the transformative journey of introspection, providing insights and practices inspired by Saint Michael to deepen self-awareness and align with our higher purpose.

The Divine Blueprint: Understanding Humanity's Creation in the Image of God through Saint Michael's Wisdom

The Spark of Divinity: "In His Image"

Genesis 1:27 – The Foundation of Divine Resemblance

Genesis 1:27 is a profound starting point for understanding human nature in Judeo-Christian thought: "So God created mankind in his own image, in the image of God he created them; male and female he created them." This verse speaks not merely of physical likeness but of a spiritual blueprint, imparting qualities such as creativity, moral reasoning, and an inner capacity for love, justice, and compassion.

Through the lens of Saint Michael, this divine resemblance is a call to align with the qualities that connect us to the divine while also recognizing our potential for error. As protector and guide, Saint Michael emphasizes the importance of nurturing these divine attributes, both to fulfill our purpose and to find balance within ourselves and the world around us. Humanity, created with divine resemblance, possesses unique traits: the ability to discern right from wrong, create from the depths of imagination, and pursue wisdom—all qualities Michael upholds and encourages in those he guides.

Saint Michael's Perspective: Guardianship over Humanity's Divine Nature

Saint Michael's connection to humanity's divine image is deeply rooted in his role as a guardian and intercessor. As the protector of light and truth, Michael recognizes the potential in humanity to act as both creators and caretakers of creation. However, this role is also one of great responsibility, one that Michael reminds us requires reverence, humility, and self-discipline.

According to teachings found in *The Midrash Tanhuma*, a collection of homiletic teachings in Jewish tradition, humanity's divine nature is emphasized as the ability to walk in alignment with God's will. This suggests that within each person lies a capacity to cultivate virtues that align with cosmic order and divine truth—qualities Michael both embodies and encourages. Michael's presence serves as a constant reminder to honor this divine image, not as an abstract concept, but as a lived truth expressed in daily choices and inner attitudes.

The Life of Adam and Eve: The First Humans and the Divine Challenge

In the apocryphal text, *The Life of Adam and Eve*, we find a narrative that explores humanity's divine nature from a different angle. In this account, Adam and Eve's fall highlights the weight of free will and the struggle inherent in maintaining the purity of the divine image. This story reveals the human inclination to reach beyond boundaries, to seek knowledge that may either elevate or corrupt.

Saint Michael's role in this story is one of guidance and correction. The text recounts Michael comforting Adam and Eve after their fall and helping them find a path to redemption. For Michael, humanity's divine image is never irreparably tarnished; instead, it requires restoration through humility, introspection, and, ultimately, a commitment to truth. In his guidance, Michael represents both the strength and mercy of divine justice, offering a path for humanity to return to its intended nature.

Honoring the Divine Image: A Ritual of Self-Recognition

To connect more deeply with the divine image within, consider performing a ritual that invites Saint Michael's guidance, using his protective presence to explore and honor your divine attributes. This ritual is designed to help you internalize these qualities, purify self-perception, and align with the virtues that reflect divine likeness.

Ritual Preparation

- **Setting**: Choose a quiet, sacred space where you feel at peace. You may wish to create an altar with symbols of Saint Michael, such as a small sword, a blue or white candle, and a mirror to represent reflection and self-recognition.

- **Materials**:
    - A white or blue candle (symbolizing divine light and Michael's guidance)
    - A small mirror
    - A bowl of water (for purification)
    - Frankincense or sandalwood incense (to create a sacred atmosphere)
    - A notebook or journal for reflection

Step-by-Step Ritual Instructions

1. Centering and Invocation

Begin by lighting the incense and the candle, focusing on your breath as you center yourself. Imagine a protective circle of light forming around you, inviting Saint Michael's presence to guard and guide you. Place your hand over your heart and say:

"Saint Michael, Archangel and protector, I call upon you to guide me in understanding my own divine nature. Help me to see myself as God sees me, to recognize the qualities that connect me to the divine, and to purify anything that clouds this vision."

2. Reflection on the Divine Image

Hold the mirror in your hands, looking into your own eyes. As you gaze into the mirror, imagine yourself not as you are, but as a divine creation, carrying the potential for wisdom, compassion, and truth. Reflect on *Genesis 1:27*:

"I am created in the image of God, holding within me a spark of the divine."

Take a moment to reflect on what this means personally. Think of qualities you admire that reflect this divine nature—kindness, resilience, creativity, courage. Allow yourself to embrace these qualities as part of who you are.

3. Cleansing and Reclaiming

Dip your fingers in the bowl of water and gently touch your forehead, heart, and hands, saying:

"I cleanse myself of any thoughts or feelings that do not honor the divine image within me. I release all doubt, fear, and judgment."

Close your eyes and picture Saint Michael's light flowing over you, purifying and renewing you. Feel his protective energy enveloping you, allowing you to let go of any lingering negativity or self-doubt. This step symbolizes the commitment to honor your highest self and to release what no longer serves you.

4. Affirming Divine Qualities

Take a moment to identify one or two qualities you wish to strengthen, such as compassion, honesty, or courage. Speak these qualities aloud, affirming your intention to embody them:

"Saint Michael, grant me the strength to embody [compassion, honesty, courage, etc.]. May I live as a reflection of the divine image within me, guided by truth and integrity."

As you speak, visualize each quality filling you, like light entering your heart and radiating outward. Imagine Saint Michael beside you, his sword raised, reinforcing these qualities within you.

5. Closing the Ritual

To close, thank Saint Michael for his guidance and protection. Extinguish the candle, symbolizing the completion of the ritual but the continuation of the divine light within. Place your hands together in gratitude, saying:

"Thank you, Saint Michael, for helping me see the divine within myself. May I walk forward with courage and grace, honoring this image in all I do."

Integrating the Divine Image: Practices for Daily Life

After performing this ritual, the journey of embodying the divine image continues in daily practice. Saint Michael teaches that living in alignment with the divine image requires dedication, mindfulness, and inner discipline. Here are ways to integrate these lessons:

1. **Daily Reflection**
   Each morning, take a few moments to remind yourself of the qualities you wish to embody. Consider keeping the mirror from your ritual as a symbolic reminder, reflecting your commitment to self-awareness and divine alignment.
2. **Regular Self-Examination**
   In the spirit of Psalm 139: "Search me, O God, and know my heart," examine your thoughts and actions throughout the day. When challenges arise, ask yourself how you can respond in a way that reflects the divine image within you. Saint Michael's guidance can be summoned in moments of temptation or confusion, reminding you of your higher purpose.
3. **Embodying Compassion and Courage**
   Saint Michael, as a figure of strength and compassion, encourages acts of kindness, patience, and courage. Look for opportunities to express these qualities in your interactions, seeing each act as a reflection of divine likeness.
4. **Journaling with Intent**
   At the end of each day, journal briefly about any moments when you felt connected to your divine nature or experienced challenges. Reflect on how you responded and any insights you gained. This practice

strengthens the link between inner awareness and outward action.

A Lasting Transformation: Walking in Divine Light

The journey to understanding and embodying humanity's divine image is lifelong, and Saint Michael's teachings serve as a compass. Through ritual, reflection, and intentional action, you open yourself to a greater understanding of what it means to carry the divine image within, to act with integrity, and to live as a force of compassion and truth in the world. In honoring this inner likeness to the divine, you not only uplift yourself but become a channel for Michael's protective and guiding light, a true reflection of the divine order in the universe.

Choosing Light: Free Will and the Battle Between Good and Evil through Saint Michael's Guidance

The Power of Choice: "Life and Death, Blessings and Curses"

In the Book of Deuteronomy, the concept of free will is framed as a choice between life and death, blessings and curses. Deuteronomy 30:19-20 states:

"This day I call the heavens and the earth as witnesses against you that I have set before you life and death, blessings and curses. Now choose life, so that you and your children may live."

This declaration serves as both an invitation and a directive. God presents humanity with the freedom to choose, urging individuals to "choose life" by following a path of wisdom, compassion, and righteousness. Saint Michael, known as the

Archangel of divine justice and protector of truth, is a steadfast guide in this journey of choice. His presence reinforces the notion that while each person has the power to choose, choices are not without consequence. In his teachings, Saint Michael emphasizes choosing the path of light and virtue over darkness and despair.

The Book of Enoch: Spiritual Influences on Human Free Will

The *Book of Enoch*, an apocryphal text, provides a dramatic exploration of free will, especially in its depiction of spiritual beings influencing humanity. This ancient text describes the "Watchers"—a group of angels who descended to Earth and influenced human behavior. They introduced humanity to knowledge both enlightening and corrupting, leading to a heightened awareness of good and evil.

Saint Michael's role within the *Book of Enoch* is clear: he acts as the defender of divine order, countering the chaos introduced by the Watchers and guiding humanity toward spiritual alignment. In this narrative, he embodies both justice and mercy, actively intervening to restore balance and protect the integrity of human choice. His involvement serves as a reminder that while humanity is subject to influences, both seen and unseen, the power of choice remains intact, and Saint Michael's guidance can help steer individuals toward paths aligned with divine purpose.

The Guardian of Free Will: Saint Michael's Role in Guiding Choices

Saint Michael's role in the battle between good and evil is not simply as a warrior against external darkness but as a guide who reinforces the inner struggle between light and shadow within each soul. His teachings emphasize that free will is a sacred responsibility and that each choice brings one closer to divine light or further into darkness.

Michael's guidance can be seen as the voice that urges discernment, reminding us to consider the spiritual consequences of each choice. In times of moral uncertainty or when confronted with temptation, his presence encourages individuals to align with higher virtues and resist impulses that may lead to harm. In his role as protector, Michael exemplifies strength, integrity, and courage, qualities he encourages us to embody in our choices. His presence in our lives acts as a constant reminder to pursue paths of honesty, compassion, and resilience against forces—both internal and external—that may sway us from our true calling.

Ritual of Discernment: Seeking Michael's Guidance in Choosing Light

To deepen your connection with Saint Michael and strengthen your ability to choose light over darkness, consider performing a ritual dedicated to discernment. This ritual will help you clarify your intentions, fortify your will, and invite Michael's protective influence to guide you in making choices aligned with divine light and truth.

Preparation for the Ritual

- **Setting**: Select a peaceful, sacred space where you feel safe and focused. Create an altar with symbols of Saint Michael, such as a small sword or shield, a blue candle, and any objects that represent courage and integrity to you.
- **Materials**:
    - A blue or white candle (representing Saint Michael's protective light)
    - A small mirror (for self-reflection)
    - A bowl of water (symbolizing purity and clarity)
    - Frankincense incense (for spiritual clarity)
    - A notebook or journal for insights and reflections

Step-by-Step Ritual Instructions

1. Centering and Invocation of Saint Michael

Begin by lighting the candle and incense. Close your eyes and take deep breaths, centering yourself. Imagine a protective circle of light around you, calling forth Saint Michael's presence to join you. Place your hands over your heart and say:

"Saint Michael, Archangel of divine truth and protector of all who seek the light, I call upon you to guide me in understanding my choices. Help me to choose paths that align with goodness, truth, and integrity. Protect me from influences that would lead me astray and empower me to see with clarity and courage."

2. Reading and Reflection on Free Will

Reflect on *Deuteronomy 30:19-20*, repeating it aloud slowly:

"This day I call the heavens and the earth as witnesses against you that I have set before you life and death, blessings and curses. Now choose life, so that you and your children may live."

Hold the mirror in your hands and look into it. As you gaze into your own eyes, allow yourself to reflect on recent choices or areas in your life where you seek greater alignment with light and truth. Imagine Saint Michael standing beside you, reinforcing your strength to choose the highest path.

3. Cleansing and Releasing

Dip your fingers in the bowl of water, touching your forehead, heart, and hands as you say:

"I cleanse myself of confusion and any influences that obscure my path. I release all hesitation and fear, inviting only clarity and purpose in my choices."

Visualize any doubts or negative influences washing away, leaving you with a sense of purity and resolve. This step serves as a symbolic purification, preparing you to receive Michael's guidance with an open heart and mind.

4. Affirmation of Intentions and Personal Will

Take a moment to silently or aloud affirm your intention to live in alignment with your highest self. Speak words that reflect your dedication to choosing goodness, truth, and light in all actions:

"Saint Michael, I commit to living a life guided by wisdom, compassion, and truth. May my choices reflect the divine light within me, and may I always have the courage to choose what is right, even when it is difficult."

Envision a bright, protective light surrounding you, symbolizing Saint Michael's unwavering support. Allow this light to fill you, reinforcing your strength and resilience.

5. Closing the Ritual

When you feel complete, thank Saint Michael for his guidance and protection. Extinguish the candle, symbolizing the closing of the ritual but retaining the protective light within. Bow your head in gratitude, saying:

"Thank you, Saint Michael, for your wisdom and guidance. May I walk forward in strength, clarity, and light, choosing the path of goodness and resisting all darkness."

Integrating the Lessons of Free Will: Practices for Daily Life

After performing this ritual, it's essential to carry the teachings into your daily life. Saint Michael's guidance is most impactful when integrated into real-world decisions and behaviors, strengthening your commitment to choosing light consistently.

Practicing Discernment in Choices

Each day, remind yourself of the importance of choice by taking a brief moment in the morning to reflect on the power of free will. As you encounter choices, big or small, ask yourself whether each decision aligns with your highest values. Visualize Saint Michael's presence guiding your thoughts and helping you discern.

Reflecting on Influences

Throughout the day, practice noticing the influences around you—whether they are people, environments, or even your thoughts. Saint Michael teaches that we must remain vigilant about the influences that shape our choices. As a daily exercise, reflect on whether the influences in your life encourage light and growth or contribute to fear and doubt. This reflection helps you to stay aligned with your intentions.

Journaling and Self-Examination

At the end of each day, take a few minutes to journal about the choices you made, especially those that challenged you. Consider how Saint Michael's presence might have affected your decisions. Ask yourself whether your choices contributed to your sense of peace, purpose, and alignment with the divine. Use your journal as a tool for self-examination, inviting honesty and self-compassion in this process.

Choosing Light: A Lasting Journey with Saint Michael's Guidance

The battle between good and evil is not merely external; it is a deeply personal journey shaped by daily choices. Saint Michael's guidance is an invitation to honor the divine gift of free will by consistently choosing light, resisting darkness, and embracing our role as active participants in the moral fabric of creation. Through this ritual and ongoing practices, you deepen your relationship with Saint Michael and cultivate an awareness that transforms choices into opportunities for growth, alignment, and divine connection.

In honoring these teachings, you step into your own power, embodying courage, resilience, and integrity, aligned with Saint Michael's strength and protection on the path of light.

The Quest for Inner Truth: Discernment and Self-Knowledge through Saint Michael's Teachings

The Prayer of the Heart: "Search Me, O God"

Psalm 139:23-24 offers a powerful invocation of introspection:

"Search me, O God, and know my heart; test me and know my anxious thoughts. See if there is any offensive way in me, and lead me in the way everlasting."

These verses embody a vulnerable yet courageous request to be known entirely by the divine. To open one's heart to God's gaze is to invite a revealing of truths, even those difficult to confront. In the context of Saint Michael's guidance, this prayer serves as an invitation to discernment. Saint Michael, the Archangel of truth and justice, stands as a protector who urges honesty and self-knowledge. His presence is a reminder that self-awareness is a path to spiritual strength, providing clarity to our intentions, motivations, and actions.

Through Saint Michael's lens, this prayer becomes a powerful tool for reflection, helping us to recognize our divine potential while acknowledging and addressing any shadows within. It is the call to pursue truth within oneself, recognizing that to fully serve the light, one must face even the unflattering aspects of their being.

Pirkei Avot: Wisdom in Knowing Oneself

In *Pirkei Avot* (Ethics of the Fathers), an essential text in Jewish thought, the importance of self-awareness is emphasized as a foundation for wisdom. One of its teachings states, "Know from where you came and to where you are going." This guidance encourages a lifelong journey of self-discovery and responsibility, urging individuals to align their actions with a greater purpose.

Saint Michael's approach aligns with the wisdom of *Pirkei Avot* by emphasizing self-knowledge as a precursor to discernment. When one understands their inner nature, they are better prepared to make choices that align with truth and justice. Michael's guidance encourages us to go beyond surface awareness, delving into the motivations, beliefs, and inner desires that shape our actions. By understanding these influences, we can act with intention and integrity, embodying a life that resonates with divine principles.

Saint Michael's Perspective: The Role of Introspection and Self-Awareness

Saint Michael values introspection not as a form of self-judgment, but as a means of fortifying the soul. In his teachings, self-awareness is the foundation of spiritual resilience. By knowing oneself, one becomes more resistant to external temptations and more aligned with inner truth. Michael's role as a protector is mirrored in his encouragement of self-knowledge, urging us to be honest with ourselves so that we may live in alignment with divine will.

In times of self-doubt or confusion, Michael's presence can be felt as a grounding force, guiding us to examine our thoughts and feelings without fear. Through his lens, self-awareness becomes an act of courage—facing our shadows and bringing them into the light of understanding. By acknowledging both our strengths and weaknesses, we empower ourselves to grow spiritually and walk a path of integrity.

Guided Meditation on Introspection and Self-Awareness: A Journey within with Saint Michael

This meditation practice, inspired by Saint Michael, is designed to open the heart and mind to self-knowledge, fostering an honest connection with one's inner self.

Preparation for Meditation

- **Setting**: Choose a calm, comfortable space free from distractions. Consider creating a small altar or space that includes a blue candle (for clarity and truth) and an object symbolizing Michael's protective energy, such as a small sword or shield.
- **Materials**:
  - A blue candle (to represent Michael's clarity and guidance)
  - A mirror (for self-reflection)
  - A journal for recording insights after the meditation
  - Optional: incense like frankincense to create a serene atmosphere

Step-by-Step Meditation Instructions

1. Centering and Invoking Saint Michael

Light the blue candle and sit comfortably, placing the mirror in front of you. Close your eyes and take several deep breaths, allowing your mind and body to settle. Picture a gentle light surrounding you, infused with Saint Michael's protective and clarifying presence.

Say aloud or in your mind:

"Saint Michael, guardian of truth and protector of the soul, I invite your presence as I journey within. Help me to see myself with honesty and compassion, and guide me in understanding the truths within my heart."

2. Reflection on Psalm 139

Begin by reflecting on the verses of Psalm 139:23-24:

"Search me, O God, and know my heart; test me and know my anxious thoughts. See if there is any offensive way in me, and lead me in the way everlasting."

Allow these words to resonate within you, feeling their invitation to explore without fear or judgment. As you reflect, imagine a light surrounding your heart, representing Saint Michael's energy, giving you the strength to face any truths that may arise.

3. Gazing into the Mirror: Self-Reflection

Open your eyes and look gently into the mirror before you. As you gaze into your reflection, let go of any self-judgment. See yourself as you are, without any masks or expectations. Imagine that you are seeing yourself through Saint Michael's eyes—full of compassion, strength, and understanding.

Say:

"Saint Michael, help me to see the divine within myself and to recognize the shadows that I must face. I seek truth with an open heart."

Take a few minutes to gaze into the mirror, allowing any thoughts or feelings to arise naturally. You may notice specific memories, emotions, or patterns coming forward. Acknowledge them without attachment, simply observing.

4. Inner Dialogue: Listening to Your Heart

Close your eyes and shift your focus to your heart. Visualize it as a source of inner wisdom, connected to the divine. Mentally ask yourself, "What do I need to know about myself?" or "What truths do I need to face?"

Sit quietly and listen to any responses that arise. These may come as words, images, or feelings. Trust that whatever arises is what you need to hear at this moment. Feel Saint Michael's presence as a steady, protective force, offering reassurance.

5. Affirming Self-Awareness

After reflecting, affirm your commitment to self-awareness and growth. Say:

"Saint Michael, I thank you for your guidance in seeing myself clearly. May I walk in truth, with courage to grow and wisdom to choose the light."

Visualize yourself filled with a radiant light that carries both understanding and compassion. Imagine this light integrating into your being, strengthening your self-awareness and alignment with truth.

6. Closing the Meditation

Gently open your eyes. Extinguish the candle, thanking Saint Michael for his presence. Spend a few moments in silence, letting the insights settle within you.

Additional Practices for Self-Awareness from Saint Michael's Teachings

In addition to this meditation, Saint Michael encourages regular practices that reinforce introspection, discernment, and self-compassion. Here are several daily or weekly practices that can help cultivate self-awareness in alignment with his teachings.

Morning Reflection: Starting Each Day with Clarity

Each morning, set aside a few moments to reflect on a question or intention that promotes self-awareness. For example, ask yourself, "What qualities do I want to embody today?" or "How can I remain true to my highest self?" Saint Michael's guidance can be invoked by imagining his presence with you, offering strength and clarity to face the day's challenges.

Journaling for Self-Knowledge

End each day with a brief journaling session. Reflect on moments when you felt aligned with your true self and those where you may have acted out of alignment. This practice not only reinforces self-awareness but also helps you recognize patterns and areas for growth. Imagine Saint Michael beside you as you write, guiding you toward truth and self-compassion.

Mirror Work for Self-Reflection

Use a mirror as a tool for regular self-reflection. This practice involves looking into your own eyes and speaking kindly to yourself, affirming your strengths, intentions, and growth. It's a practice rooted in self-acceptance and honesty, helping you to see yourself as you truly are. As you gaze into the mirror, imagine Saint Michael's light surrounding you, affirming the strength within you.

Acts of Courage and Compassion

Saint Michael's teachings emphasize living with courage and compassion. Each day, look for opportunities to practice these qualities—whether in difficult conversations, standing up for your beliefs, or showing kindness to yourself and others. As you integrate these actions, you become a living reflection of Saint Michael's guidance, embodying self-awareness through each choice.

Walking the Path of Truth: Integrating Self-Knowledge with Saint Michael's Guidance

The journey of self-knowledge is a continuous one, inviting us to return to ourselves with each experience. Saint Michael's teachings remind us that knowing oneself is not merely a practice but a way of life—an alignment of mind, heart, and spirit with divine truth.

Through meditation, reflection, and mindful action, you bring Saint Michael's guidance into your daily life, reinforcing self-awareness and cultivating a resilience that enables you to face the world authentically. By honoring both light and shadow within yourself, you walk in the light of truth, embodying courage, compassion, and an unwavering commitment to your highest self.

Having journeyed through the depths of self-knowledge and discernment, we now approach the teachings of divine justice, where Saint Michael's influence extends beyond personal transformation to the broader cosmic order. If self-awareness and truth guide our inner lives, divine justice directs our relationships with others and the world itself. Rooted in compassion, balance, and accountability, divine justice emphasizes restoration rather than retribution, seeking to heal and realign rather than condemn. Through the wisdom of scriptures, Jewish teachings on *Tikkun Olam*, and apocryphal accounts, Saint Michael emerges not merely as a warrior but as a steward of divine harmony, emphasizing justice tempered with mercy and spiritual correction. With these principles, Saint Michael guides us in understanding the interwoven nature of actions and consequences, encouraging us to act justly and restore balance. We now move forward into an exploration of divine justice, uncovering how justice, mercy, and restoration shape the path toward a more harmonious existence.

2. The Path of Divine Justice: Restoration, Mercy, and Spiritual Balance through Saint Michael's Guidance

In the realm of divine justice, Saint Michael's teachings illuminate the profound principles that guide our moral and spiritual responsibilities toward one another and the world. Unlike a justice rooted in retribution, Saint Michael exemplifies a justice that seeks restoration, encouraging us to learn, correct, and heal. Anchored in the sacred call to "do right" as voiced in Isaiah, the wisdom of Tikkun Olam (the Jewish concept of repairing the world), and teachings on mercy and accountability, Saint Michael's approach balances strength with compassion. His role as a guide, defender, and intercessor underscores the importance of mercy in judgment, recognizing that each action carries spiritual consequences and opportunities for growth. In exploring justice as a path to divine harmony, Saint Michael teaches us to embody mercy, embrace accountability, and become instruments of healing and balance. Through these teachings, we delve into how justice—tempered with mercy—becomes a transformative force for both individual and collective upliftment.

The Sacred Art of Justice: Restoration over Punishment in Saint Michael's Teachings

Seeking True Justice: "Learn to Do Right, Seek Justice"

Isaiah 1:17 calls out to the heart of divine justice with a simple yet profound directive:

"Learn to do right; seek justice. Defend the oppressed. Take up the cause of the fatherless; plead the case of the widow."

This verse embodies the spirit of justice as envisioned in sacred texts—a justice that goes beyond punishment to seek righteousness, compassion, and restoration. In this view, justice serves to uplift, heal, and realign rather than condemn or retaliate. Saint Michael's approach to justice echoes this call. As the Archangel of divine order and cosmic balance, he guides us toward a justice that transcends mere retribution, focusing on healing, unity, and the restoration of peace.

When Isaiah speaks of "learning" justice, it implies that justice is an evolving practice, requiring both wisdom and humility. In Saint Michael's perspective, this justice is not passive or removed but actively compassionate, requiring discernment and understanding of the circumstances that lead to imbalance or harm. Justice, in this sense, becomes an opportunity for both the wronged and the wrongdoer to realign with divine principles and recognize the sacred in one another.

Tikkun Olam: The Power of Restoration in Jewish Tradition

The Jewish concept of *Tikkun Olam*, or "repairing the world," aligns closely with Saint Michael's vision of justice. *Tikkun Olam* holds that humanity has a sacred responsibility to heal and repair the world through acts of compassion, justice, and kindness. This concept goes beyond individual acts of justice, seeing each contribution as part of a greater, ongoing process of cosmic restoration. Just as a fractured vase can be pieced back together to create something new, *Tikkun Olam* teaches that every act of justice brings creation closer to its intended harmony.

Saint Michael's role in *Tikkun Olam* is twofold: he acts as a protector of this cosmic order, preserving balance, and as a guide, urging individuals to partake in this divine work of restoration. In his role, he embodies *Tikkun Olam* by showing us that our actions, especially those that repair or uplift, carry spiritual weight that reverberates across time and space. His presence reminds us that justice begins with a recognition of interconnectedness and shared responsibility, inspiring us to see the divine in all and to act with reverence toward one another.

Saint Michael's Role in Restoring Balance: Insights from The Ascension of Isaiah

In the apocryphal text *The Ascension of Isaiah*, Saint Michael is portrayed as a protector and guide who helps restore order when chaos or imbalance threatens the spiritual world. This text illustrates Michael's role in battling dark forces that attempt to disrupt divine harmony. However, rather than fighting simply to defeat evil, Michael's purpose is to reinstate the natural order, reminding us that justice, in his perspective, is a return to harmony.

The *Ascension of Isaiah* presents Saint Michael as a being who strives to protect both earthly and heavenly realms, underscoring that justice is a restorative act that preserves the balance of creation. His battles are not merely struggles against evil forces but efforts to bring wayward forces or beings back into alignment with divine law. In this way, Michael's view of justice is both compassionate and firm—offering the chance for redemption and healing while defending the sanctity of divine order.

A Ritual of Restoration: Inviting Saint Michael's Guidance in Practicing Justice

In honoring Saint Michael's approach to justice as restoration, consider a ritual dedicated to aligning with the principles of compassion, healing, and restoration. This ritual aims to foster an understanding of justice that reflects divine compassion, seeing justice not as an opportunity for punishment but as a means of restoring balance.

Preparation for the Ritual

- **Setting**: Choose a quiet, comfortable space that feels sacred to you. Set up an altar with symbols of justice and restoration, such as a white or blue candle, a small bowl of water (symbolizing purity), and a plant or leaf (representing growth and renewal).
- **Materials**:
    - A blue or white candle (to invoke Michael's guidance)
    - A bowl of water (for cleansing and renewal)
    - A green or white cloth to represent harmony and balance
    - Frankincense or myrrh incense (for purity and sacred intention)
    - A journal or notebook for reflections

Step-by-Step Ritual Instructions

1. Centering and Invocation of Saint Michael

Begin by lighting the candle and incense. Close your eyes, taking deep, steady breaths to center yourself. Visualize a sphere of light surrounding you, infused with Saint Michael's presence and energy, protecting you with compassion and strength.

Place your hand over your heart and say:

"Saint Michael, Archangel of divine justice and balance, I invite you to guide me in understanding justice as a path of restoration and healing. Help me to act with compassion, to seek justice that heals, and to bring balance where there is discord."

2. Reflection on Isaiah 1:17

Read Isaiah 1:17 aloud:

"Learn to do right; seek justice. Defend the oppressed. Take up the cause of the fatherless; plead the case of the widow."

Allow these words to resonate, contemplating the idea of justice as an act of compassion. Reflect on areas in your life or within yourself where you might bring about healing or balance, whether through forgiveness, understanding, or a change in perspective. Imagine Saint Michael standing beside you, reinforcing your resolve to approach justice as a healer and protector.

3. Purification and Intention-Setting

Dip your fingers in the bowl of water and touch your forehead, heart, and hands, symbolizing the cleansing of your thoughts, feelings, and actions. Say:

"I purify myself of judgment, bitterness, or harshness. May my heart seek only justice that restores, justice that heals, and justice that uplifts."

Picture any negative thoughts or emotions dissolving into the water, leaving you with a sense of clarity and renewal. This step is designed to align your intentions with Saint Michael's view of compassionate justice, preparing you to act with both mercy and integrity.

4. Affirming Justice as Restoration

Place the green or white cloth before you, representing harmony. Hold your hands over the cloth, focusing on the qualities you wish to embody in your approach to justice—compassion, understanding, and strength. Speak aloud:

"Saint Michael, grant me the strength to seek justice as a force of restoration. Help me to defend the vulnerable, to act with compassion, and to restore balance wherever it is needed."

Imagine a wave of peace and balance flowing from Saint Michael through you, filling you with a renewed sense of purpose. Feel this energy grounding you, guiding your sense of justice toward acts that heal rather than harm.

5. Closing the Ritual

When you feel complete, close the ritual by thanking Saint Michael for his guidance and protection. Extinguish the candle, symbolizing the completion of the ritual and the ongoing light of justice within you. Bow your head in gratitude, saying:

"Thank you, Saint Michael, for guiding me on the path of justice and restoration. May I carry your teachings into my life, seeking to heal, uplift, and restore balance wherever I go."

Integrating the Teachings of Restorative Justice into Daily Life

After this ritual, allow Saint Michael's approach to restorative justice to guide your daily actions and decisions. Justice, when practiced in the spirit of restoration, becomes a continuous journey that touches all aspects of life. Here are practices inspired by Saint Michael's teachings to help integrate this perspective.

Practicing Compassionate Judgment

In daily interactions, remember the distinction between punishment and restoration. When conflicts arise, approach them with a mindset that seeks to understand and heal rather than judge or condemn. Visualize Saint Michael's presence reinforcing your ability to view situations with a compassionate eye.

Acts of Service and Restoration

Embrace opportunities for acts of service, especially those that uplift others or repair relationships. Whether by supporting a friend, volunteering, or reconciling with someone, each act of kindness becomes a step in *Tikkun Olam*, healing the world through love and justice.

Reflecting on Balance and Harmony

End each day with a brief reflection on where you contributed to balance and harmony. Journal about moments where you acted with compassion and understanding, and consider areas where you might need further alignment. This practice, inspired by Michael's teachings, helps you stay mindful of justice as a path of restoration.

The Path Forward: Living Justice as a Restorative Force

Saint Michael's vision of justice is one of profound compassion and strength, seeing beyond punishment to focus on healing and renewal. When we embrace justice as an opportunity to restore, we act as agents of peace, unity, and divine harmony. Through rituals, daily reflections, and acts of compassion, we can embody Saint Michael's teachings, weaving justice into our lives as a sacred force for good.

As we move forward, we step onto the path of divine justice with renewed purpose, empowered by the wisdom of Isaiah's call to "seek justice" and guided by Michael's unwavering commitment to balance and restoration.

The Mercy Within Justice: Saint Michael's Embodiment of Compassionate Justice

"Act Justly, Love Mercy, Walk Humbly": Micah's Call to Integrate Justice with Mercy

In Micah 6:8, a timeless call to live ethically and compassionately resonates:

"He has shown you, O mortal, what is good. And what does the Lord require of you? To act justly and to love mercy and to walk humbly with your God."

This verse offers a profound synthesis of divine justice, underscoring that true justice is inseparable from mercy and humility. Acting justly and loving mercy is the essence of divine compassion, urging humanity to wield justice with empathy, even for those who have erred. In Saint Michael's teachings, justice is not merely a strict balancing of deeds but a means of guiding individuals back to alignment with their highest nature. Michael, as the defender of truth and guardian of divine order, embodies this justice balanced by mercy. Through his role as protector, he both defends against darkness and extends mercy to those seeking redemption, embodying a compassionate and dignified justice that is transformative rather than punitive.

Mercy as Essential to Justice: Insights from Talmud Berakhot

The Talmudic teachings, particularly in *Berakhot*, emphasize that mercy is not just a component but the very heart of divine justice. In Jewish wisdom, justice without mercy risks becoming rigid and devoid of the warmth necessary for human flourishing. Mercy, then, tempers justice, ensuring that it remains compassionate and responsive to the unique needs of each individual.

Saint Michael's embodiment of this Talmudic wisdom reminds us that justice without compassion is incomplete. He guides us toward a perspective that seeks to understand the human spirit's struggles, offering mercy as an opportunity for growth and healing. In this light, Michael teaches that every act of justice should be informed by mercy—a reflection of divine love that acknowledges human imperfection while encouraging transformation. For those who seek his guidance, Michael's teachings reveal that mercy is not a weakness within justice but a strength that uplifts and restores.

Saint Michael's Compassionate Justice: Guiding without Judgment

As an archangel, Saint Michael's role extends beyond simply enforcing cosmic law; he is also a patient guide, defending without condemnation. His justice is therefore not punitive but protective and supportive, aimed at aligning beings with divine purpose. Michael does not judge harshly but seeks to restore and guide, even when confronting darker forces. His protection is inherently compassionate, safeguarding the dignity of all souls and inviting them to embrace their highest potential.

This approach reflects Michael's deep commitment to divine mercy as an integral part of justice. Through his actions, he teaches that each individual is worthy of both accountability and compassion, showing that mercy within justice fosters redemption rather than resentment. To embody Michael's way of justice is to walk a path that protects, restores, and heals, all without casting judgment. It's a reminder that true strength lies in helping others return to the light, giving them the guidance and protection they need to overcome darkness.

Ritual of Compassionate Justice: Inviting Saint Michael's Guidance to Embody Mercy

In practicing compassionate justice as taught by Saint Michael, this ritual is designed to align your sense of justice with mercy and understanding. It allows you to reflect on the interconnectedness of justice and mercy, invoking Saint Michael's guidance to help you extend compassion in moments of judgment or conflict.

Preparation for the Ritual

- **Setting**: Select a quiet space that feels sacred and calming. Create an altar or setup that includes symbols of Saint Michael and mercy, such as a blue or white candle, a feather (representing gentleness), and a bowl of salt water (symbolizing purification).
- **Materials**:
    - A blue candle (symbolizing Saint Michael's compassionate justice)
    - A small bowl of salt water (for purification and renewal)
    - Lavender or rose incense (to create a gentle, serene atmosphere)
    - A small mirror (for self-reflection)
    - A notebook or journal for reflections and insights

Step-by-Step Ritual Instructions

1. Centering and Invoking Saint Michael

Light the blue candle and the incense, allowing yourself to enter a calm, focused state. Close your eyes, taking slow, deep breaths, and visualize a soft blue light surrounding you. This light represents Saint Michael's protective presence, embodying both justice and mercy.

Place your hand over your heart and say:

"Saint Michael, Archangel of justice and mercy, I invite your guidance to show me the way of compassionate justice. Help me to see others with understanding, to offer mercy within justice, and to protect with love rather than judgment."

2. Reflecting on Micah 6:8

Slowly read Micah 6:8 aloud:

"To act justly and to love mercy and to walk humbly with your God."

Allow these words to settle into your heart. Reflect on times when you've felt called to act justly and extend mercy. Consider moments when you may have judged yourself or others harshly. Imagine Saint Michael's presence beside you, offering you both strength and compassion to soften judgment without sacrificing integrity.

3. Cleansing with Salt Water

Dip your fingers in the salt water and gently touch your forehead, heart, and hands, symbolizing a cleansing of thoughts, emotions, and actions. Say:

"I cleanse myself of harsh judgment and open myself to the way of compassionate justice. May I act with strength and mercy, seeing others as worthy of understanding and respect."

Visualize the water purifying any judgments or tensions, leaving you with a sense of renewal. This cleansing step invites you to align with Michael's view of justice as a path to healing and restoration, preparing you to embody these qualities.

4. Gazing into the Mirror: Self-Reflection

Hold the mirror before you, looking gently into your own eyes. As you gaze, invite Saint Michael's guidance to help you see yourself with compassion and honesty. Reflect on any judgments you may hold toward yourself and allow them to soften. Imagine that you are seeing yourself as Saint Michael sees you, with acceptance, patience, and hope.

Say:

"Saint Michael, teach me to see myself and others with kindness. May my judgments be fair and my heart be open to mercy, walking humbly in the light of justice."

Take a few minutes to observe any thoughts or emotions that arise. Let yourself feel Saint Michael's protective energy surrounding you, reinforcing your commitment to practicing mercy within your pursuit of justice.

5. Affirming Compassionate Justice

Place your hand over your heart, focusing on the qualities of mercy, humility, and strength. Speak these words:

"Saint Michael, I affirm my commitment to justice that is tempered by mercy. May I seek understanding before judgment and offer compassion without weakness. May my actions reflect the balance of justice and mercy that you embody."

Visualize Saint Michael's light filling you with these qualities, merging strength and compassion within you. Feel this light anchoring in your heart, preparing you to carry it forward in your actions and interactions.

6. Closing the Ritual

To close, thank Saint Michael for his guidance and presence. Extinguish the candle, symbolizing the completion of the ritual and the ongoing light of compassionate justice within. Take a deep breath and bow your head, saying:

"Thank you, Saint Michael, for teaching me the way of justice and mercy. May I carry your guidance into my life, seeking to protect, heal, and restore without judgment."

Integrating Compassionate Justice into Daily Life

After completing this ritual, the teachings of Saint Michael on mercy within justice can be woven into everyday life. Practicing compassionate justice requires ongoing reflection, humility, and openness, qualities that can transform both personal and social interactions.

Practicing Forgiveness and Understanding

Each day, look for opportunities to offer forgiveness, whether to yourself or others. Saint Michael's way of justice calls for empathy before judgment, and practicing forgiveness fosters a sense of understanding and peace. As you do, imagine Saint Michael's presence reinforcing your ability to forgive and release resentment.

Reflecting on Justice with Compassion

At the end of each day, take a few moments to reflect on any judgments or decisions you made. Consider how mercy may have shaped your actions differently. This practice, inspired by Michael's teachings, encourages self-awareness and reinforces the integration of mercy within justice.

Extending Kindness in Small Interactions

Even small acts of kindness can reflect Michael's vision of compassionate justice. Whether offering a listening ear, supporting someone in need, or practicing patience in difficult situations, each act becomes a manifestation of mercy and strength. These moments remind you that justice, in its highest form, restores rather than divides.

The Transformative Power of Justice Rooted in Mercy

To live by Saint Michael's teachings on compassionate justice is to walk a path of both strength and grace. Mercy within justice transforms how we view ourselves and others, inviting us to act with empathy while upholding integrity. Through rituals, daily reflections, and acts of kindness, you embody Michael's vision of justice that protects, uplifts, and restores.

As you move forward, let Micah's call to "act justly, love mercy, and walk humbly" resonate in your heart, with Saint Michael as a steadfast guide. In embracing mercy as a powerful force within justice, you align with a divine path that heals, nurtures, and brings balance to a world in need of both compassion and courage.

The Path of Consequence: Divine Justice and Spiritual Correction through Saint Michael's Teachings

"You Reap What You Sow": The Principle of Cause and Effect in Galatians

The principle of spiritual consequence is powerfully expressed in Galatians 6:7:

"Do not be deceived: God cannot be mocked. A man reaps what he sows."

This verse speaks to the universal law of cause and effect, underscoring that actions bear inevitable results, and these results align with the nature of those actions. In the view of divine justice, this is not about punishment but rather a fundamental truth of spiritual growth. Actions aligned with love, wisdom, and integrity yield blessings, while those rooted in harm or dishonesty create challenges or obstacles for the soul.

Saint Michael, as a champion of divine justice, embodies this principle by guiding individuals through the consequences of their choices with both strength and compassion. His teachings encourage self-reflection on the impact of one's actions, understanding that each choice shapes one's spiritual path. Through Michael's perspective, we learn that consequences are not mere retribution but an opportunity for spiritual growth. Each consequence offers a chance to realign with divine will and transform areas of one's life that require greater awareness or integrity.

The Wisdom of Solomon: Consequence as a Teacher

The *Wisdom of Solomon*, a text that dives into the nature of virtue and divine wisdom, teaches that the soul learns through experience and correction. The concept of "consequence as a teacher" is rooted in the understanding that the soul is strengthened, not weakened, by facing the results of its actions. Just as a gardener prunes a tree to encourage growth, divine justice allows individuals to face the outcomes of their choices, ensuring that each lesson is internalized and integrated.

Saint Michael's role in guiding souls through their consequences is akin to the wisdom of a mentor who helps shape one's growth by encouraging self-awareness. Michael's influence supports those willing to learn, presenting consequences as lessons rather than punishments. Under his guidance, the soul is encouraged to see its errors without shame, to understand the spiritual law at work, and to accept responsibility for its growth. Through this perspective, each consequence becomes a stepping stone toward wisdom, humility, and alignment with divine will.

Saint Michael as Intercessor and Corrector of Souls: Insights from Apocryphal Texts

In apocryphal texts, Saint Michael often appears as an intercessor who mediates between the divine and humanity. One such example is his role in *The Apocalypse of Paul*, where Michael intercedes on behalf of souls undergoing judgment. Here, Saint Michael's intervention is not to negate the consequences of actions but to provide guidance and compassion, helping souls understand their errors and return to the path of light.

Michael's role as a corrector of souls is grounded in mercy, as he seeks to guide individuals toward redemption without condemnation. He serves as a divine advocate, emphasizing correction as an act of love rather than judgment. This portrayal of Saint Michael as intercessor illustrates that divine justice, as he embodies it, offers not only balance but also the possibility of transformation. By helping individuals see their actions in the light of truth, Michael encourages them to embrace accountability, thus setting the soul on a path of healing and spiritual resilience.

Ritual of Spiritual Correction: Embracing Saint Michael's Guidance on Consequence and Growth

This ritual is intended to align oneself with the principles of consequence and spiritual correction as taught by Saint Michael. It provides a space for self-reflection, helping individuals understand their actions, embrace the lessons of their consequences, and seek Michael's guidance in realigning with divine intention.

Preparation for the Ritual

- **Setting**: Choose a quiet, private space where you can reflect without interruption. Create a small altar or

sacred area with symbols of Saint Michael, such as a blue candle, a feather, and a clear quartz crystal to symbolize clarity and self-reflection.
- **Materials**:
    - A blue candle (for Michael's guidance and clarity)
    - A small bowl of saltwater (for purification)
    - A feather or small stone (to represent lightness and grounding in truth)
    - Frankincense incense (for spiritual clarity)
    - A journal or notebook for reflections and insights

Step-by-Step Ritual Instructions

1. Centering and Invocation of Saint Michael

Begin by lighting the blue candle and incense. Close your eyes, taking deep breaths, allowing yourself to enter a state of calm and receptivity. Visualize a sphere of protective light surrounding you, inviting Saint Michael's presence.

Place your hands over your heart and say:

"Saint Michael, guardian of justice and truth, I invite your guidance to help me see my actions clearly and embrace the lessons they offer. Help me to accept responsibility, seek growth, and align my life with the divine light."

2. Reflection on Galatians 6:7

Slowly read Galatians 6:7 aloud:

"Do not be deceived: God cannot be mocked. A man reaps what he sows."

As you meditate on these words, allow their meaning to unfold within you. Reflect on areas of your life where you may be experiencing consequences. See each outcome not as punishment but as an invitation to grow, an opportunity to realign with your highest self. Imagine Saint Michael beside you, reinforcing your ability to face these consequences with courage and humility.

3. Cleansing and Preparation with Salt Water

Dip your fingers in the bowl of salt water, touching your forehead, heart, and hands as a symbol of cleansing. Say:

"I purify myself of fear and resistance. May I see my actions with clarity, accept my consequences with grace, and embrace the lessons they offer."

Visualize the water dissolving any feelings of shame or fear, leaving you open to the insights and healing that come from accepting the natural outcomes of your actions.

4. Self-Reflection on Consequences

Hold the feather or stone in your hands, grounding yourself in the present moment. Close your eyes and take a few deep breaths, connecting to your heart. Reflect on the following questions:

- What actions have I taken recently that are bearing fruit—whether positive or challenging?
- What lessons are these consequences revealing about my intentions, patterns, or beliefs?

Sit quietly with these reflections, allowing your mind to wander over the past days, weeks, or months. As insights arise, feel Saint Michael's compassionate presence supporting you, reinforcing the idea that every consequence, whether pleasant or difficult, is a stepping stone toward wisdom.

5. Embracing the Lesson with Saint Michael's Guidance

After reflecting, hold your hands over your heart and speak the following affirmation:

"Saint Michael, I embrace the lessons of my actions and seek to grow through my choices. Help me to act with awareness and integrity, aligning with the divine order and sowing seeds of love, wisdom, and compassion."

Picture a light expanding from your heart, filling you with clarity and a renewed sense of purpose. Imagine this light radiating outward, symbolizing your commitment to act with greater understanding and alignment in all areas of your life.

6. Closing the Ritual

Thank Saint Michael for his guidance, acknowledging the importance of spiritual correction in your journey. Extinguish the candle, symbolizing the completion of the ritual and your dedication to learning from your actions. Say:

"Thank you, Saint Michael, for guiding me on the path of truth and justice. May I carry your wisdom into my actions, embracing every consequence as an opportunity for growth and alignment."

Integrating Spiritual Correction into Daily Life

After completing this ritual, the teachings of Saint Michael on spiritual correction and consequence can be woven into your daily actions and reflections. Embracing the principle of "you reap what you sow" with mindfulness and integrity helps create a life aligned with divine order.

Reflecting on Actions and Intentions

Each morning, set an intention to be mindful of your actions, recognizing that each choice has the potential to sow seeds of growth. At the end of each day, take a few minutes to reflect on whether your actions aligned with your highest intentions and consider any lessons from the consequences you've observed.

Practicing Accountability with Compassion

Accountability, when practiced with compassion, becomes a transformative tool for growth. When you notice areas for improvement, commit to positive change without judgment. Saint Michael's teachings remind us that we are all learning, and each mistake can be a pathway to wisdom when faced openly and honestly.

Embracing Responsibility with Gratitude

View the natural consequences of your actions with gratitude, even when they bring challenges. Each consequence offers valuable insight into your inner world, helping you understand how your choices impact yourself and others. By embracing responsibility, you empower yourself to act consciously and with a heart open to divine guidance.

Moving Forward: Aligning with the Wisdom of Consequence and Correction

To embody Saint Michael's teachings on consequence and spiritual correction is to understand that every choice shapes our journey. This awareness transforms consequences into opportunities for learning, healing, and growth. Through this ritual and daily practices, you deepen your relationship with divine justice, seeing every action as part of a greater tapestry woven with intention, consequence, and correction.

With Saint Michael as a steadfast guide, you walk a path that honors the wisdom of sowing and reaping, embracing the lessons that come from each experience. In this way, you align with the law of divine justice, becoming a conscious co-creator in the unfolding of your highest potential.

Capstone Ritual: The Embodiment of Divine Justice through Saint Michael's Guidance

This final ritual serves as a culmination of the teachings on divine justice explored throughout this chapter. It is a practice of embodying Saint Michael's guidance and integrating the lessons of restoration, mercy, and spiritual correction into your life. Unlike the previous rituals, this one focuses on quiet reflection, visualizations, and a sense of completion, allowing you to internalize and commit to living out these principles in your daily actions.

Purpose of the Ritual

This ritual marks the end of your journey through the teachings of Saint Michael on divine justice. It aims to:

1. Integrate the lessons of justice, mercy, and accountability into your being.
2. Symbolize your commitment to carry Saint Michael's compassionate justice forward in all aspects of life.
3. Create a lasting, personal connection with Saint Michael, inviting his continued guidance in your path toward truth and harmony.

Unique Symbolism and Setting

To mark this ritual as a sacred closure, choose a unique symbol that resonates with you as a representation of Saint Michael's teachings on justice. This could be:

- A small stone or crystal (e.g., lapis lazuli for wisdom or clear quartz for clarity).
- A symbolic item from nature, such as a feather (for balance and protection) or a leaf (for growth and renewal).

Place this item on your altar along with the materials used in previous rituals, such as a blue candle and a bowl of water with salt, representing purity and transformation. The altar should feel complete, signifying the unity of all the lessons learned.

Step-by-Step Ritual Instructions

1. Simple Invocation and Centering

Begin by lighting the blue candle and incense if desired. Close your eyes, take deep breaths, and feel yourself connecting to the quiet, steady presence of Saint Michael. As you center yourself, hold your symbolic item and let it represent the culmination of the journey, a tangible reminder of Saint Michael's guiding presence.

Say:

"Saint Michael, Archangel of divine justice and truth, I call upon you now to help me embody the lessons of justice, mercy, and compassion. Guide me to live in harmony with your teachings, seeking truth, balance, and restoration."

Allow a moment of silence, feeling Michael's presence and support surrounding you.

2. Reflection on the Path of Justice

Hold the symbolic item in your hands as you reflect on the three main principles explored in this chapter:

- **Restoration Over Retribution**: Recall what it means to practice justice as a path of healing rather than punishment. Reflect on how you can continue to bring balance and peace to situations in need of justice.
- **Mercy as a Strength in Justice**: Think of moments when you've shown or received mercy, embracing it as a transformative force. Consider how you can continue

to practice justice with compassion and understanding.
- **Accountability and Consequence**: Recognize the spiritual importance of accepting the consequences of actions. Reflect on how you might strengthen your commitment to personal responsibility and growth, aligning your life with truth and integrity.

As you hold these reflections in your mind, imagine each principle filling your symbolic item with light, creating a vessel that embodies Saint Michael's teachings.

3. Visualization: Walking with Saint Michael

Close your eyes and visualize yourself in a calm, open space. Imagine Saint Michael standing beside you, radiating a light of strength, protection, and compassion. In this vision, he guides you through scenes from your daily life, showing how you can integrate his teachings into your interactions, decisions, and reflections.

See yourself acting with clarity, balance, and compassion in each situation he presents. Visualize this as a peaceful yet powerful reminder that justice guided by Saint Michael is restorative, merciful, and transformative.

Take your time in this visualization, allowing the experience to feel vivid and real, as if Saint Michael is truly walking with you, offering guidance and support.

4. Sealing the Commitment

With your symbolic item still in hand, speak aloud a commitment to live according to the principles of divine justice as taught by Saint Michael. Say:

"With Saint Michael as my guide, I commit to embodying the path of divine justice. May my actions reflect mercy, my decisions bring restoration, and my heart remain aligned with truth. Let this symbol be a reminder of Saint Michael's teachings and my commitment to carry them forward."

Place the item in a place where you will see it often, such as your altar, a bedside table, or another sacred spot. Let it serve as a touchstone for the values of justice and mercy, reminding you of your commitment to integrate Saint Michael's teachings into your life.

5. Simple Closing and Gratitude

When you feel complete, close the ritual by extinguishing the candle, representing the integration of Saint Michael's light into your inner being. Bow your head, saying:

"Thank you, Saint Michael, for guiding me on the path of justice. May I walk forward in alignment with your teachings, seeking to heal, protect, and restore wherever I go."

Sit in quiet reflection for a few moments, feeling the completeness of the ritual and the presence of Saint Michael's support.

Moving Forward: Daily Integration of Saint Michael's Teachings

Now that the ritual is complete, carry Saint Michael's guidance with you. Use your symbolic item as a reminder of your commitment, holding it during moments of reflection or decision-making to center yourself in his teachings.

Brief Reflection Practice

Each morning, briefly hold your symbolic item and recall one of Saint Michael's principles to carry with you for the day, such as mercy or accountability. At the end of the day, reflect on how this principle showed up in your actions, relationships, or inner thoughts. Journaling these reflections can deepen your understanding and ongoing connection with Michael's teachings.

Walking in Harmony with Saint Michael's Path of Justice

By completing this ritual, you have embraced the teachings of Saint Michael on divine justice, committing to live with compassion, accountability, and strength. With your symbolic item as a reminder, continue to integrate his principles into your daily life. With each action aligned with his teachings, you honor Saint Michael's guidance and bring light, justice, and healing into the world.

As we conclude our exploration of divine justice through Saint Michael's teachings, we now turn our attention to the vast and intricate design of *Cosmic Truths*. In this new chapter, we delve into the underlying principles that unite creation, examining the cosmic interplay of light and shadow, and the cycles of order and chaos that shape existence. These teachings, illuminated by Saint Michael's guidance, reveal a universe bound together by divine intent, where all things are interconnected, purposeful, and balanced. Moving from the individual path of justice to the grander scale of universal truths, we will explore how Saint Michael perceives the unity of creation, his role in harmonizing opposing forces, and his guardianship over the cosmic rhythms that sustain life. Through these reflections, we come to understand the sacred architecture of the cosmos and our place within its profound, harmonious design.

3. Cosmic Truths: Understanding the Unity, Balance, and Cycles of Creation through Saint Michael's Teachings

In this exploration of Cosmic Truths, we venture into the vast interconnected web that forms the fabric of creation, guided by Saint Michael's perspective on divine unity and balance. These teachings reveal that the cosmos is not a collection of isolated parts but a living whole, bound together by divine intention. We will begin by examining the unity of all creation, understanding how each part contributes to a greater harmony as described in Colossians and the Zohar. From there, we will delve into the balance of light and shadow as essential elements in the divine plan, where Saint Michael acts as a mediator between these forces. Finally, we explore the cosmic cycles of order and chaos, discovering how these rhythms bring about growth, renewal, and transformation. Together, these cosmic principles illuminate a deeper understanding of Saint Michael's role in the universe, helping us see how we, too, participate in this vast, unfolding divine harmony.

The Unity of All Creation: Saint Michael's Vision of Cosmic Interconnectedness

"In Him All Things Hold Together": The Binding Force of Creation in Colossians

The concept of universal unity, as expressed in Colossians 1:16-17, illuminates a profound truth about the interconnectedness of all existence:

"For in him all things were created: things in heaven and on earth, visible and invisible... all things have been created through him and for him. He is before all things, and in him all things hold together."

This passage reveals that creation is neither random nor fragmented; it is purposefully crafted and sustained by a divine force that binds all parts into a cohesive whole. Every star, every soul, and every atom exists in divine unity, each piece an integral part of a harmonious cosmic design. For Saint Michael, this unity is a fundamental principle of the cosmos—a binding truth that forms the foundation of divine justice, balance, and purpose.

Saint Michael's teachings invite us to recognize that we are not isolated beings but interconnected parts of a vast, divine tapestry. He guides us to see this unity as an ever-present reality, reminding us that our actions, thoughts, and intentions resonate beyond ourselves. Like notes in a symphony, each individual contributes to the resonance of the whole, echoing the presence of the divine within and around us. In this understanding, the cosmos is not simply a backdrop to human life but an active, vibrant field of divine expression, where each element holds a purpose and significance within the grander scheme.

The Zohar on Cosmic Interconnectedness: A Jewish Mystical Perspective

The *Zohar*, a foundational text in Jewish mysticism, delves deeply into the unity and interdependence of all things within creation. According to the *Zohar*, each part of existence reflects and influences the other; nothing exists in isolation. This mystic text describes the divine light as a continuous stream that connects and nourishes every layer of creation, from the highest spiritual realms down to the physical world. Through this divine stream, all beings are interwoven into a single fabric, their energies and destinies interconnected by the flow of divine will.

In Saint Michael's teachings, this mystical unity is seen as part of the divine order he protects and upholds. Just as each angel, soul, and element of nature has a role within this order, so too does every human being play a unique part in maintaining harmony. This perspective encourages us to act in ways that honor our interconnectedness, knowing that our choices affect not only our lives but also the lives of others and the balance of creation itself.

Saint Michael's Perspective on the Unity of the Cosmos: Insights from The Book of Enoch

In *The Book of Enoch*, an apocryphal text filled with accounts of angelic hierarchy and cosmic order, Saint Michael appears as a guardian who protects both earthly and heavenly realms. His role extends beyond that of a warrior; he is a mediator of divine harmony, maintaining the structure that allows all beings to coexist in a balanced whole. In this vision of the cosmos, Saint Michael stands as a protector of the sacred unity, ensuring that each being's purpose aligns with divine will.

The *Book of Enoch* portrays Michael as a guide who helps souls understand their place within the larger cosmic framework. In moments when chaos or imbalance threatens, Michael acts to restore order, realigning wayward forces with the divine plan. His presence and influence underscore that unity is not passive—it is actively sustained through intention, compassion, and commitment to the sacred balance.

Ritual of Unity: Embracing the Interconnectedness of All Creation with Saint Michael's Guidance

This ritual is designed to connect you to the divine unity of all creation, helping you experience your place within the interconnected fabric of the cosmos. Inspired by Saint

Michael's teachings, this practice aligns your awareness with the sacred harmony he protects and fosters.

Preparation for the Ritual

- **Setting**: Find a quiet space where you feel connected to the natural world. If possible, perform this ritual outdoors, or bring natural elements like plants, stones, or a bowl of water into your space to symbolize the unity of all life.
- **Materials**:
    - A blue or white candle (symbolizing the divine light of unity)
    - A small bowl of water (representing the fluid, interconnected flow of life)
    - A piece of natural material, like a feather or stone (to remind you of your connection to the earth)
    - Incense, such as sandalwood or cedar (to evoke a sense of sacred space and connection)
    - A notebook or journal for reflections and insights

Step-by-Step Ritual Instructions

1. Simple Centering and Invocation of Saint Michael

Begin by lighting the candle and incense, allowing the space to fill with the scent and light. Sit comfortably and close your eyes, taking several deep breaths. Imagine a warm light encompassing you, connecting you to everything around you. This light represents the unity of creation, the energy that binds all things together.

Say:

"Saint Michael, protector of divine unity, I invite your presence here. Help me to see and feel my connection to all creation, to understand the divine harmony that binds all things. May I recognize my place within this unity and act with love, respect, and purpose."

Allow yourself to feel the presence of Saint Michael as a guide and protector, a being who upholds the order and unity of the cosmos.

2. Reflecting on Colossians 1:16-17

Slowly read Colossians 1:16-17 aloud:

"In him all things hold together."

Let this verse resonate in your heart. Reflect on what it means for all things to be held together within the divine, from the smallest particle to the largest star. Think of how every aspect of existence is connected and interdependent. Imagine your own life as a thread woven into this cosmic tapestry, each action and intention affecting the greater whole.

3. Visualization: Experiencing Cosmic Unity

Close your eyes and hold the piece of natural material, such as a feather or stone, in your hands. Visualize yourself standing in the center of a vast network of light that extends endlessly in all directions. Each point of light represents a being, an element, or a soul, all interconnected by streams of energy. Feel your own light as part of this intricate web, linked to every other being.

See Saint Michael standing beside you, his presence radiating a steady strength and compassion. In this visualization, imagine him showing you how each thought, action, and feeling reverberates through the network, touching and affecting others. Allow yourself to feel the profound sense of connection, knowing that you are part of something infinitely greater than yourself.

4. Setting an Intention for Unity

Place your hands over your heart and, holding onto the sense of interconnectedness, set an intention to honor this unity in your daily life. Speak this intention aloud:

"I am one with all creation. May I act with love, compassion, and awareness of my connection to all beings. With Saint Michael's guidance, may I live in harmony with the divine unity that sustains and surrounds me."

Feel this intention sinking into your heart, becoming a commitment to act with respect for the interconnected web of life.

5. Closing the Ritual

To close, thank Saint Michael for his guidance and protection. Extinguish the candle, symbolizing the integration of this unity within yourself, and place your natural item on your altar or somewhere meaningful where you can see it often. This will serve as a reminder of your connection to all creation.

Bow your head in gratitude, saying:

"Thank you, Saint Michael, for guiding me to see and honor the unity of creation. May I carry this awareness forward, seeking harmony, compassion, and love in all I do."

Integrating the Unity of Creation into Daily Life

After completing this ritual, you can continue to embody Saint Michael's teachings on unity by practicing mindful awareness of your connection to all beings.

Daily Reflection on Unity and Connection

Begin each day with a brief moment of reflection, reconnecting to the unity of all creation. Visualize the network of light, reminding yourself that your actions and thoughts resonate beyond yourself. Take this awareness into your interactions and decisions, seeking to act in ways that support and uplift others.

Extending Compassion in Small Interactions

Each interaction becomes an opportunity to honor the unity of creation. Whether through a kind word, a small act of help, or a moment of listening, view each connection as a reflection of the greater whole. These small acts remind you of your place in the cosmic network and the impact you have on others.

Journaling Moments of Connection and Awareness

Each evening, journal about moments in your day when you felt connected to others or the world around you. Reflect on how this awareness of unity influences your choices and how it brings a sense of purpose and peace to your life. Journaling helps solidify the teachings of Saint Michael, making the unity of creation a lived reality.

Embracing the Unity of Creation as a Path of Spiritual Fulfillment

To live in alignment with Saint Michael's teachings on unity is to embrace the profound interconnectedness that binds all of existence. Through this awareness, you become a conscious participant in the cosmic harmony, recognizing the divine in every interaction, every choice, and every moment. By embodying this unity, you walk in step with Saint

Michael, acting as a guardian of balance, compassion, and purpose within the sacred web of life.

The Balance of Light and Shadow: Saint Michael's Role in the Divine Plan

"The Light Shines in the Darkness": Understanding the Divine Dance of Light and Shadow

In John 1:5, we find the powerful declaration:

"The light shines in the darkness, and the darkness has not overcome it."

This verse reflects the profound truth that light and darkness coexist as part of the divine order, each with its own purpose and significance. The light, as described in the Gospel of John, symbolizes divine wisdom, love, and the presence of God's truth that guides and uplifts all beings. Darkness, on the other hand, is often perceived as the unknown, the challenges, or the trials we face. However, from a higher perspective, darkness is not a force opposed to light but rather a field in which light can shine all the brighter, making the divine presence visible even amid trials.

For Saint Michael, the balance of light and shadow is a central element of his role as guardian and protector. In his teachings, he emphasizes that light is not meant to eliminate shadow; rather, shadow provides the contrast through which the beauty, resilience, and strength of light can be fully realized. This balance allows us to experience life's depth, to grow through challenges, and to embrace the transformative power of both joy and sorrow, clarity and mystery.

Kabbalistic Interpretations of Light and Shadow: Harmony within the Divine Plan

In Kabbalistic tradition, light and shadow are not antagonistic but complementary forces within the divine creation. Kabbalistic teachings explore the idea that the universe is formed from both "revealed" light and "hidden" light, the latter often appearing as shadow or mystery. This concept aligns with the Kabbalistic Tree of Life, where different spheres or *sefirot* represent varying manifestations of divine energy, from mercy and wisdom to judgment and restraint. Each of these elements is essential, forming a harmonious system that reflects the complete nature of the Divine.

According to Kabbalistic wisdom, light is the energy of creation, clarity, and revelation, while shadow represents the unknown, the latent potential waiting to be understood. In this context, shadow is not something to be feared or avoided but to be acknowledged and embraced as part of the path to enlightenment. Saint Michael's role, therefore, is not only to protect us from destructive darkness but to guide us in navigating these contrasts, helping us find clarity within obscurity and purpose within difficulty.

Saint Michael's Role in Balancing Forces of Light and Darkness

As an archangel, Saint Michael embodies the delicate balance between light and shadow, serving as a divine protector who guards against forces that seek to disrupt this equilibrium. He does not seek to eradicate shadow, for he understands that both light and shadow are woven into the fabric of creation. Instead, Michael's role is to uphold the harmony between these forces, ensuring that each serves its purpose within the divine plan.

In times of struggle, confusion, or darkness, Saint Michael is there to remind us of the light within ourselves and the purpose of our trials. His guidance allows us to navigate through shadows, understanding that every experience—whether filled with light or shadow—serves a higher purpose. By helping us integrate both aspects into our lives, Saint Michael leads us to a more holistic understanding of existence, one in which all things, even challenges and fears, contribute to our spiritual growth.

Ritual for Embracing Light and Shadow in Divine Balance

This ritual is designed to help you align with the balance of light and shadow as taught by Saint Michael. Through this practice, you'll learn to honor both aspects as essential elements of the divine plan, recognizing that each has a role in guiding, transforming, and elevating your soul.

Preparation for the Ritual

- **Setting:** Perform this ritual in a space where you can dim the lights and create both light and shadow within the room. This could be done indoors with a single candle or outdoors in the early evening when natural light begins to fade.
- **Materials:**
    - A single white or blue candle (representing the light of divine truth)
    - A small, dark-colored cloth or object (to symbolize shadow and the mysteries it holds)
    - Incense, such as frankincense or myrrh, to create a sacred, reflective atmosphere
    - A mirror (for self-reflection and to symbolize the integration of light and shadow within you)
    - A notebook or journal for insights and reflections

Step-by-Step Ritual Instructions

1. Centering and Invoking Saint Michael's Presence

Begin by lighting the candle and incense, creating a space where light and shadow coexist. Dim the lights or allow dusk to create natural shadows in the room. Close your eyes, taking several deep breaths to center yourself. Feel the stillness around you and visualize a soft, protective light surrounding your space.

Place your hand over your heart and say:

"Saint Michael, guardian of divine balance, I invite your presence to guide me. Help me to embrace both light and shadow, to understand the divine purpose in each, and to walk in harmony with the sacred balance of creation."

As you feel Michael's presence, let yourself relax, trusting in his guidance and protection throughout the ritual.

2. Reflection on John 1:5

Slowly read John 1:5 aloud:

"The light shines in the darkness, and the darkness has not overcome it."

Contemplate this verse, allowing its meaning to resonate within you. Think of moments in your life where light and shadow have intersected—times when challenges revealed deeper truths, or when sorrow led to growth. Imagine how these experiences, while difficult, contributed to your understanding, resilience, and spiritual depth.

3. Embracing the Symbolism of Light and Shadow

Hold the candle in one hand and the dark-colored cloth or object in the other. Visualize the candle as your inner light—the divine wisdom, clarity, and love within you. See the dark cloth as the unknown, the aspects of life and self that remain hidden or mysterious.

Say aloud:

"I honor both light and shadow as parts of the divine plan. In light, I find clarity and purpose; in shadow, I find growth and mystery. Together, they create a balance within me, revealing the fullness of who I am."

As you speak these words, envision a sense of peace between these two forces. See them not as opposites but as partners in the dance of existence, each enhancing the other's purpose.

4. Mirror Reflection: Integrating Light and Shadow within Yourself

Place the mirror in front of you and gaze into your own eyes. Reflect on how light and shadow coexist within you—your strengths and joys, your fears and challenges. Recognize that both aspects are part of your path, each contributing to your spiritual evolution.

Say:

"Saint Michael, help me to see the divine light within my shadows and to honor the mystery within my light. May I walk in balance, embracing both aspects of myself with understanding and love."

Spend a few minutes in quiet reflection, allowing insights or emotions to arise as you gaze into the mirror. Let this reflection deepen your understanding of how both light and shadow shape who you are.

5. Setting an Intention to Live in Balance

Place your hands over your heart, focusing on the sense of balance created by embracing both light and shadow. Speak an intention to carry this awareness into your daily life:

"With Saint Michael's guidance, I commit to honoring the balance of light and shadow within and around me. May I find strength in the light and wisdom in the shadow, walking in harmony with the divine plan."

Feel this intention becoming a part of your being, grounding you in the understanding that every experience—whether bright or dark—holds value and meaning.

6. Closing the Ritual

To close, thank Saint Michael for his guidance and protection. Extinguish the candle, symbolizing the integration of light and shadow within you, and bow your head in gratitude.

Say:

"Thank you, Saint Michael, for guiding me in understanding the sacred balance of light and shadow. May I carry this awareness with humility, courage, and compassion."

Sit in quiet reflection for a few moments, feeling the harmony of light and shadow within yourself before moving from your sacred space.

Integrating Light and Shadow into Daily Life

After completing this ritual, continue to embrace Saint Michael's teachings by recognizing and honoring the roles of light and shadow in your everyday experiences.

Morning Intention Setting: Honoring Both Aspects of Self

Each morning, set an intention to honor both light and shadow within yourself and in others. Acknowledge that every person and situation holds elements of both, and seek to approach each interaction with an open heart that embraces the totality of existence.

Reflective Practice: Finding the Lesson in Challenges

During times of difficulty, pause to reflect on how the current shadow or challenge may be revealing hidden strength, wisdom, or clarity. Visualize Saint Michael by your side, helping you to see through the darkness to the lessons and growth opportunities it offers.

Journaling the Balance of Light and Shadow

At the end of each day, journal about moments of light and shadow, noting what each has taught you. This practice reinforces Saint Michael's guidance to view challenges as transformative and strengths as pathways for greater compassion.

Embracing the Dance of Light and Shadow

Living in alignment with Saint Michael's teachings on light and shadow means embracing life in all its complexity. By honoring both forces, we find greater resilience, understanding, and compassion. Light reveals truth, while shadow brings depth, helping us to walk in balance with the divine order. Through reflection, intentionality, and guided practices, we integrate Saint Michael's wisdom into our lives, becoming vessels of harmony, strength, and purpose.

Cycles of Divine Order and Chaos: Saint Michael's Wisdom on the Rhythms of Creation

"A Time for Everything": Ecclesiastes on the Rhythmic Flow of Life

In *Ecclesiastes 3:1-8*, a timeless passage speaks to the heart of life's inherent rhythms:

"To everything there is a season, and a time for every matter under heaven: a time to be born, and a time to die; a time to plant, and a time to pluck up what is planted; a time to kill, and a time to heal..."

This verse reveals the ebb and flow of existence, suggesting that life unfolds in a sequence of opposing yet complementary forces. These cycles are not random; they represent the divine order in which every phase has its role and purpose. This cycle between creation and destruction, growth and decay, order and chaos is part of a greater cosmic rhythm that ultimately sustains balance in the universe.

For Saint Michael, these cycles are manifestations of divine wisdom. He teaches that each stage, whether we perceive it as positive or challenging, holds significance in the grand design. Rather than resisting these shifts, Saint Michael invites us to accept and flow with them, seeing change as a divine tool for growth and evolution. In his teachings, he emphasizes that true peace and resilience come from aligning with these cosmic rhythms, honoring both order and chaos as parts of the sacred journey.

Sefer Yetzirah and the Cycles of Cosmic Order

In *Sefer Yetzirah*, one of the foundational texts in Jewish mysticism, creation is described as structured around dynamic cycles and energies. According to this text, everything in the universe exists within an intricate framework of elements, numbers, and seasons that give rise to continuous change and renewal. This cyclical nature is what maintains balance, not only in the external world but also within the human soul. The constant movement between order and chaos is seen as essential to the vitality of existence, allowing the divine to reveal itself in new forms.

From Saint Michael's perspective, this cosmic order does not imply rigidity. Instead, it represents a harmonious interplay where chaos introduces new possibilities and order provides stability. By embracing this dance, we learn to see chaos not as destruction but as the necessary energy that breathes life into new creations, much like how a field must be tilled—disrupted—to prepare for new seeds. Saint Michael encourages us to see ourselves as participants in this cycle, both creating and surrendering, to fulfill our spiritual potential.

Saint Michael's Role in Guiding Through Cycles of Order and Chaos

As a guardian of divine order, Saint Michael's role extends to balancing the forces of stability and transformation. He serves as a guide who helps souls navigate these shifting tides, showing them how to maintain integrity and courage amid life's natural upheavals. When we face periods of disorder, Michael's presence brings clarity and assurance that chaos is not an ending but a transition. In moments of harmony, he reminds us to prepare for future changes, understanding that life's still waters often precede new movements.

Through his teachings, Saint Michael encourages us to honor each stage of life, recognizing that both peace and disruption play critical roles in our spiritual evolution. With his guidance, we can approach each phase not with resistance but with acceptance and adaptability, aligning ourselves with the rhythm of divine timing.

Ritual for Embracing Divine Cycles of Order and Chaos

This ritual is designed to help you connect with and honor the cycles of order and chaos in your life, bringing a sense of balance and acceptance to the continuous changes you experience. Inspired by Saint Michael's teachings, this practice will help you see each phase as sacred, finding peace and purpose in the ebb and flow of existence.

Preparation for the Ritual

- **Setting**: Perform this ritual in a place where you can feel grounded, such as near a window where you can see nature or in a quiet space where you feel connected to the elements.
- **Materials**:
    - A white candle (symbolizing divine order and clarity)
    - A dark-colored candle (representing the mysteries of chaos and transformation)
    - A bowl of earth or soil (to ground you in the cycles of growth and decay)
    - Incense, such as sage or cedar, to purify and connect with the sacred
    - A small, symbolic item that represents a past challenge you have overcome (this will serve as a reminder of resilience through change)
    - A journal or notebook for reflections and insights

Step-by-Step Ritual Instructions

1. Centering and Invocation of Saint Michael

Begin by lighting the incense to cleanse the space, letting the smoke rise and swirl, creating an atmosphere of reflection. Light both the white and dark candles, placing them side by side to symbolize the balance of order and chaos.

Place your hand over your heart, close your eyes, and say

"Saint Michael, guide of divine order, protector through times of change, I invite your presence. Help me to embrace the cycles of life with faith and courage, seeing each phase as sacred and purposeful. May I walk with trust in both the calm and the storm, knowing I am guided by divine timing."

Imagine Saint Michael's light surrounding you, bringing a sense of peace and readiness to journey through the cycles of life.

2. Reflection on Ecclesiastes 3:1-8

Slowly read Ecclesiastes 3:1-8 aloud:

"To everything there is a season, and a time for every matter under heaven…"

Reflect on this verse, contemplating the times in your life that have felt like "planting" and "harvesting," "tearing down" and "building up." Consider how each phase, whether joyful or challenging, contributed to your growth and understanding. Visualize each cycle as a season in your spiritual journey, knowing that both order and chaos have shaped who you are.

3. Embracing the Symbolism of Order and Chaos

Hold the white candle in one hand and the dark-colored candle in the other. Take a deep breath and meditate on the nature of order and chaos, seeing them not as opposites but as partners in the rhythm of creation. Picture the white candle as the steadying force that provides structure and clarity, and the dark candle as the energy of transformation that breathes new life into old patterns.

Say aloud:

"I honor both order and chaos in my life, knowing that each has its purpose in the divine plan. In times of peace, I find stability and clarity; in times of change, I find growth and transformation. With Saint Michael's guidance, I embrace the cycles of life with trust and resilience."

Feel the balance between these forces within yourself, allowing any resistance to change to dissolve, replaced by an acceptance of life's natural rhythm.

4. Connecting with Earth: Grounding in the Cycles of Life

Place your hands on the bowl of earth or soil, symbolizing your connection to the natural cycles of growth and decay. Imagine your life as a seed that grows, blossoms, fades, and returns to the earth to nourish future growth. Feel the groundedness that comes from understanding your place within these cycles.

Say:

"As the earth knows its seasons, I too honor the cycles within my life. I release fear of change, embracing each phase with gratitude and patience. May I walk in harmony with the divine rhythm, finding peace in every season."

Take a few deep breaths, feeling the grounding energy of the earth stabilizing you as you embrace the beauty of life's continuous flow.

5. Reflecting on Past Transformation

Hold the symbolic item that represents a challenge or transformation you have previously faced. Remember how you grew or learned from that experience, recognizing it as part of your personal cycle of growth and renewal.

Speak these words:

"With Saint Michael's guidance, I have journeyed through change and emerged renewed. May I continue to meet each cycle with courage, seeing both joy and challenge as steps on my path."

This step reinforces your ability to adapt and grow, no matter the phase of life you are in.

6. Setting an Intention for Future Cycles

Place both candles together, merging their light, and set an intention to honor the cycles of order and chaos in your life with grace and trust.

Speak this intention aloud:

"I commit to embracing the cycles of life, knowing that both order and chaos have their roles in my journey. With Saint Michael's guidance, may I face each phase with wisdom, patience, and peace."

Feel this intention anchoring within you, preparing you to navigate life's changes with acceptance and understanding.

7. Closing the Ritual

To close, thank Saint Michael for his guidance and protection. Extinguish the candles, one at a time, symbolizing the integration of both order and chaos within yourself. Bow your head in gratitude, saying:

"Thank you, Saint Michael, for guiding me in understanding the cycles of divine order and chaos. May I carry this wisdom forward, finding peace in every season of life."

Sit quietly for a few moments, reflecting on the ritual's insights before moving from your sacred space.

Integrating the Cycles of Order and Chaos into Daily Life

After completing this ritual, practice integrating Saint Michael's teachings by becoming more aware of life's natural rhythms and responding to them with trust and adaptability.

Daily Reflection: Noticing the Cycles of Your Day

Each day, take a moment to notice the small cycles of order and chaos around you. Observe how tasks, conversations, and even emotions follow a flow, with periods of stability and moments of disruption. By becoming aware of these mini-cycles, you cultivate an appreciation for the rhythms of life, reinforcing your connection to the cosmic order.

Embracing Change as a Teacher

When faced with unexpected changes or challenges, pause and remember that chaos is a necessary part of growth. Visualize Saint Michael by your side, helping you to see the lessons and opportunities within the disruption. This perspective transforms difficult moments into valuable learning experiences, aligning with Michael's teachings on embracing the divine rhythm.

Journaling Cycles of Growth and Renewal

At the end of each week, journal about experiences that felt like new beginnings or conclusions, reflecting on how they contributed to your spiritual growth. Consider how you responded to these cycles and any insights that arose. This practice helps you align with the understanding that life's transitions are part of a larger, divine order.

Walking in Harmony with the Cycles of Life

To live in alignment with Saint Michael's teachings on the cycles of divine order and chaos is to embrace the rhythm of creation with an open heart. Both stability and transformation play essential roles in the journey, guiding us through growth, renewal, and understanding. By honoring each phase with trust and resilience, you embody Michael's wisdom, becoming a vessel of peace, adaptability, and sacred balance in a world of constant change. Through reflection, awareness, and intentional living, you align with the divine dance of order and chaos, finding harmony in the ever-evolving tapestry of existence.

Saint Michael's Guardianship over Cosmic Cycles: Maintaining Balance Across the Divine Rhythms

Michael as the Guardian of Balance: Harmonizing the Cosmic Tides

Saint Michael is not merely a warrior or defender; he is a divine custodian who ensures the equilibrium of cosmic cycles—guiding both the visible and invisible forces in creation. In his role, Michael acts as the gatekeeper of divine harmony, balancing the energies of order and chaos, light and shadow, life and death. He upholds the eternal rhythm in which all things rise and fall, grow and decay, creating a cohesive balance that sustains the cosmos.

These cosmic cycles echo through all of existence, from the turning of seasons to the shifts within our souls. For Saint Michael, balance is not about preventing change but about preserving the integrity of divine timing and purpose. He teaches that all cycles, no matter how challenging or transformative, serve the divine plan, contributing to the growth, healing, and evolution of all beings. By aligning ourselves with this balance, we move in harmony with life's natural rhythms and learn to appreciate the sacred wisdom inherent in both beginnings and endings.

The Wisdom of Cycles in Sacred Texts: The Duality of Continuity and Transformation

Scriptural references, particularly in the Bible, reflect the concept of divine cycles and the importance of balance in creation. Ecclesiastes 3:1-8, which speaks of a time for everything, embodies this truth. This passage does not imply static existence but acknowledges that life's cycles are dynamic and vital to spiritual growth. Similarly, in mystical Jewish texts like the *Sefer Yetzirah*, we see creation's constant interplay of order and chaos. The text describes creation as bound by seasons, numbers, and elemental forces, all of which mirror the cyclical nature of life and the cosmos.

Michael's guardianship is an embodiment of this sacred balance. He ensures that each cycle unfolds within its intended time, creating a rhythm that sustains harmony. His teachings encourage us to witness and accept the cyclical nature of all things, knowing that every experience is part of a larger, unified design. In this view, even what we perceive as chaos is part of a greater order, a transformative energy that fosters growth, release, and renewal.

Saint Michael's Role in Guiding Souls Through Life's Cycles

Saint Michael's guidance is essential in helping souls navigate the ups and downs inherent in life's cycles. When we face periods of upheaval, confusion, or loss, Michael reminds us that these experiences are not obstacles but phases in a greater journey. His presence brings stability and assurance, helping us see beyond immediate challenges to understand the divine order at work. Just as Michael defends against threats to the cosmic order, he also helps individuals find balance within themselves, teaching us to embrace the ebb and flow of life's transformations with faith and courage.

Michael's teachings suggest that alignment with these cycles brings resilience. He instructs us to honor each stage—whether it's a season of growth, loss, creation, or transformation—knowing that every phase contributes to our development. This acceptance of life's rhythm allows us to navigate change without fear or resistance, trusting that each moment has its divine purpose. In Michael's view, true strength lies in embracing the entirety of the journey, recognizing that every step is guided by a cosmic wisdom that far exceeds our understanding.

Ritual for Embracing and Integrating the Cycles of Divine Balance

This final ritual is a contemplative practice designed to harmonize your spirit with the cosmic cycles of order and transformation that Saint Michael oversees. By connecting with these rhythms, you integrate the insights gained from previous practices into a unified, ongoing awareness of life's ever-evolving cycles. Unlike earlier rituals, this one emphasizes silent reflection and guided visualization to foster a deeper alignment with the eternal dance of creation.

Preparation: Brief Setup with Intentional Focus

For this ritual, you may choose a familiar space that allows for undisturbed silence. Gather the following items, though you may recall their symbolic meanings from previous rituals rather than explicitly focus on them here:

- **A white candle** representing divine clarity and order.
- **A dark-colored candle** symbolizing transformation and the mysteries within cycles.
- **A bowl of water** with a pinch of salt, symbolizing the grounding essence of earth and cosmic continuity.
- **A small natural item**, such as a leaf or stone, to represent the cycle of life and growth.

To honor the ritual's theme of cycles, place the white and dark candles beside each other, unlit at first. These items create a sacred space where you can shift into a reflective state, assisted by Saint Michael's presence.

Invocation and Intentions

Light both candles to symbolize the union of order and transformation. Take a deep breath, drawing Saint Michael's guidance inward, and silently acknowledge his presence as the eternal guardian of balance. Let your focus settle on experiencing the ebb and flow of life's cycles, surrendering to both stability and change.

"Saint Michael, protector of divine balance, I open myself to the cycles of life. Guide me in understanding the eternal rhythm of creation, and help me to embrace both peace and transformation with trust and humility."

Guided Visualization: Walking Through Life's Cycles with Saint Michael

Close your eyes and enter into a meditative space, envisioning yourself surrounded by Saint Michael's calming, protective energy. Imagine that he guides you on a gentle journey through past, present, and future cycles in your life, allowing you to see each phase as sacred and purposeful.

1. **Reflect on Past Cycles**
   With Saint Michael at your side, begin by recalling a past experience of transformation or growth. Observe

this memory from a detached yet compassionate perspective. Allow yourself to acknowledge how this experience—whether challenging or peaceful—has contributed to your journey. See it as a necessary piece of the divine cycle that shaped you, led you, and taught you something essential.

2. **Embrace the Present Cycle**
   Shift your attention to the present, feeling the grounding energy of the space you occupy. With Saint Michael's guidance, accept the current phase of your life, be it one of peace or transition. Imagine his light enveloping you, giving you the strength to embrace your path with trust and openness. Reflect on the support, clarity, and balance available to you in this moment.

3. **Envision Future Cycles**
   Now, imagine future cycles unfolding in alignment with divine purpose. See yourself navigating these phases with Saint Michael's steady guidance, feeling equipped to embrace both order and transformation. Allow a sense of peace to fill you as you contemplate the unknown, knowing that each future cycle will bring growth and renewal in its own time.

Allow this visualization to deepen, feeling the continuous, supportive rhythm of Saint Michael's guidance through every cycle. Know that this ongoing relationship with balance and change will carry you forward.

Setting an Intention of Alignment with Divine Cycles

After a few moments, bring your awareness back to the present. Place your hands over your heart, allowing your intention to rise from within:

"I am in harmony with the cycles of life. Guided by Saint Michael, I embrace both change and stability as sacred elements of my path. May I walk with courage, trust, and peace, honoring each cycle with humility and strength."

Feel this intention settling within you, becoming a quiet but profound commitment to live in balance with the cycles of order and transformation.

Concluding Symbolism: Leaving the Candles Lit

As a symbol of your continued alignment with these cycles, leave both candles burning for a time after you complete the ritual. Their combined light represents the ongoing presence of order and transformation in your life, a reminder that the journey through cycles is constant and sacred.

When you are ready, bow your head in gratitude, silently thanking Saint Michael for his unwavering guidance and for the gift of balance that allows you to navigate life's cycles with peace and strength.

Allow yourself a few quiet moments before returning to daily life, knowing that this ritual serves not as an ending, but as a continuous alignment with the eternal rhythm of existence.

Integrating the Wisdom of Cycles into Daily Life

After this ritual, integrate Saint Michael's teachings on cosmic balance into your daily life by practicing awareness and acceptance of the natural rhythms around you.

Morning Reflection: Observing Daily Cycles

Each morning, take a few moments to observe the beginning of a new day as part of life's continuous cycles. Acknowledge the fresh start each morning brings, setting an intention to honor the natural rhythms you encounter throughout the day.

Adapting with Peace in Times of Change

When life presents challenges or changes, remember the wisdom gained from this ritual. Pause and reflect on how each phase is part of a larger plan, reminding yourself that both peace and transformation serve a higher purpose. Visualize Michael's presence guiding you, reinforcing your ability to adapt with grace.

Weekly Journaling: Noticing Patterns and Growth

At the end of each week, journal about any patterns or cycles you noticed, whether they were internal (thoughts, emotions) or external (relationships, work). Reflect on how you responded to each phase and consider any insights gained about the balance of order and transformation. This practice aligns you with Michael's teachings, helping you recognize growth as part of life's cycles.

Living in Harmony with Saint Michael's Cosmic Balance

Saint Michael's teachings on cosmic cycles invite us to view life's rhythms as sacred, finding balance within every experience. By aligning with the cycles of order and transformation, we embody Michael's wisdom, becoming vessels of resilience, acceptance, and peace. Through reflection, intention, and conscious living, we harmonize with the eternal rhythm that guides creation, learning to trust that every moment, whether bright or shadowed, holds purpose within the divine plan.

As we move from exploring the cosmic balance of unity, light, and cyclical rhythms, we now turn our attention to the hidden realms—the angelic and spiritual dimensions where unseen forces and entities dwell. In this section, Saint Michael's guidance will help us understand these realms as profound extensions of divine order and mystery, connecting the visible world with the invisible. Through scripture, mystical insights, and Saint Michael's own teachings, we'll deepen our awareness of the angelic hierarchies, learn to recognize the influence of spiritual forces, and access these realms with reverence and purpose. These hidden realms offer pathways to wisdom and protection, encouraging us to engage them responsibly. To close, a capstone ritual will guide us in opening to Michael's continued presence in our lives, allowing us to carry his guidance into our ongoing spiritual journey.

4. Hidden Realms: Unveiling the Angelic and Spiritual Dimensions with Saint Michael's Guidance

In this next journey, we step into the hidden realms—the vast, layered dimensions that lie beyond the physical, where angelic beings, spiritual forces, and divine mysteries coexist and interact with our world. Guided by Saint Michael, protector and bridge between these realms, we explore how these unseen dimensions influence our lives, reveal truths, and offer pathways to spiritual growth. Through sacred texts, Kabbalistic wisdom, and Michael's own role in divine hierarchy, we gain insight into the angelic order and the presence of spiritual entities. We'll learn how to recognize and navigate these energies with clarity and respect, moving toward a responsible engagement with the hidden realms. This section concludes with a capstone ritual, preparing us to open fully to Saint Michael's guidance as we explore these realms and seek continued illumination on our spiritual path.

Understanding the Angelic and Spiritual Realms: Exploring Divine Hierarchies with Saint Michael's Guidance

The Protector of Israel: Michael's Role in Spiritual Defense

In Daniel 10:13, we encounter a profound moment where the angel Gabriel describes Saint Michael as "one of the chief princes" who came to his aid during a struggle with the "Prince of Persia." Here, Michael is depicted as a warrior and protector of Israel, symbolizing divine strength in defense of both people and spiritual principles. This scene reveals Michael as a guardian not only of individuals but of entire nations and cosmic orders. Through Michael's defense, we understand that angelic realms are not distant or detached; they are intimately connected to the lives, struggles, and spiritual welfare of humanity.

In this role, Michael is more than a warrior; he is a preserver of spiritual balance, ensuring that forces aligned with divine order are protected from chaotic or malevolent influences. When invoking Michael's protective essence in our own lives, we are not only calling for safeguarding but aligning ourselves with a force that defends righteousness and cosmic balance. This aspect of Michael's identity offers insight into the spiritual hierarchy he embodies—he is both leader and servant, answering to the divine order with a mission of perpetual guardianship.

Kabbalistic Perspectives: Hierarchies of the Angelic Realms

Kabbalah offers a structured view of angelic realms that gives us further insight into Michael's role in these hidden dimensions. The Kabbalistic model divides the spiritual universe into ten spheres, known as the *sefirot*, on the Tree of Life. These sefirot represent different divine attributes or emanations, and each is connected by pathways where angelic and spiritual beings operate. Angels in the Kabbalistic hierarchy are considered emissaries of the divine will, each with specific roles in maintaining universal balance. Within this structure, angels are arranged in various orders and roles, from those closest to the Divine Source down to those who interact with the physical world.

Saint Michael, in the Kabbalistic understanding, is associated with the *sefira* of Gevurah, or Strength, reflecting his qualities of protection, justice, and discipline. This placement situates Michael among the ranks of angels tasked with maintaining divine law and balance. Gevurah is characterized by boundaries, discipline, and the defense of sacred order, all of which align with Michael's roles as a warrior and protector. He is seen as a channel for divine strength, interceding when human strength alone cannot prevail. In a practical sense, invoking Michael in this context allows the practitioner to align with energies of protection, strength, and order, connecting with a source of resilience and spiritual fortitude.

Michael as a Mediator between Realms: His Connection to Hidden Realities

Saint Michael's connection to hidden realities goes beyond his protective duties; he is also a mediator, bridging the worlds of spirit and matter, light and shadow. This mediation role is seen in the apocryphal *Book of Enoch*, where Michael leads the angelic host in their interactions with humanity, protecting souls and preserving cosmic balance. In Enoch's vision, Michael guides souls, offering them insight into divine mysteries while ensuring that they do not become overwhelmed or misguided by forces beyond their understanding. This guardianship emphasizes Michael's compassionate and wise nature, as he helps souls navigate the unknown with courage and reverence.

Michael's role as a bridge highlights the interconnectedness of all realms, showing that our world and the angelic domains are woven together, each influencing and reflecting the other. By connecting with Michael as a guide, practitioners can begin to glimpse these hidden realms and gain wisdom from them while remaining grounded and protected. This role of mediator is particularly significant in exploring spiritual mysteries; Michael acts as a teacher and protector, guiding seekers through mystical insights and helping them integrate these understandings into their lives responsibly.

Ritual of Communion with the Angelic Realms: Guided by Saint Michael

This ritual is intended to align the practitioner with Saint Michael's energy, opening pathways to the angelic realms while ensuring protection, clarity, and reverence. Through this practice, you will invite Michael's guidance to help you experience a sacred connection with the higher spiritual realms.

Preparation: Creating Sacred Space and Gathering Materials

To begin, select a quiet, undisturbed area where you can sit comfortably and enter a state of reflection and openness.

Materials:

- A blue candle to symbolize Michael's protective energy and connection to divine strength.
- A small piece of silver or clear quartz to represent angelic purity and spiritual clarity.
- Frankincense or sandalwood incense to create a sacred atmosphere and connect to higher realms.
- A glass of water, symbolizing the fluid, receptive nature of spiritual insight.
- A notebook or journal to record any thoughts or insights received during the ritual.

Setting the Space: Begin by lighting the incense and placing the blue candle in front of you, with the piece of silver or quartz nearby. Place the glass of water to your right as a grounding element, reminding you to stay receptive and grounded as you reach toward the spiritual realms.

Invocation: Inviting Saint Michael's Guidance

Once you are seated and ready, close your eyes and take several deep, calming breaths. Focus on creating a steady, open awareness, imagining Saint Michael's protective presence surrounding you like a shield of light.

Say aloud:

"Saint Michael, defender and protector, I invite your presence here. Guide me to experience the divine mysteries with respect, humility, and clarity. Help me to connect with the angelic realms, not out of curiosity, but out of reverence for the divine order. Shield me from all harm and keep my intentions pure as I seek to understand the hidden realms."

Feel a sense of warmth and strength, as though Michael's presence fills the space around you. Imagine him standing beside you, a guardian who guides and protects as you begin this journey.

Guided Visualization: Journeying into the Angelic Realms

With Michael's presence firmly established, gently close your eyes and begin a visualization to connect with the angelic realms. Imagine yourself standing at the base of a radiant staircase that seems to ascend into light. Saint Michael stands beside you, a steady and protective presence.

1. **Ascending with Reverence** Imagine taking your first steps up the staircase with Michael beside you, each step bringing a feeling of peace and elevated understanding. The air feels pure, charged with a sense of divine purpose, and you feel a deepening connection to the angelic realms.

2. **Entering the Realm of Light** At the top of the staircase, envision a doorway filled with a soft, welcoming light. Together with Michael, step through, entering a realm where

everything radiates with purity and calm. Here, angelic beings are present, although they remain slightly obscured, allowing you only a gentle perception of their essence. Sense their warmth and wisdom, acknowledging their presence with a silent gesture of respect.

3. Receiving Guidance and Insight In this realm, open yourself to any impressions or insights. These may not come as words but rather as feelings, images, or symbols. If a question arises in your mind, mentally present it to Michael, trusting that he will help interpret any messages you may receive. Allow these impressions to come naturally without forcing any specific answer or experience.

Take your time here, absorbing any feelings of peace, protection, or understanding that arise. When you sense that this part of the journey is complete, imagine Michael guiding you back to the entrance, helping you to descend the staircase slowly, feeling grounded and calm as you return to the present moment.

Closing and Expression of Gratitude

When you have fully returned, take a deep breath, feeling the grounded energy of the space around you.

Say:

"Thank you, Saint Michael, for guiding and protecting me in this journey to the angelic realms. May I carry forward the insights gained with reverence and humility. I honor the divine order and trust in the guidance of the angelic realms."

Extinguish the blue candle and sit quietly, allowing any final thoughts or feelings to settle. If you feel inspired, write down any impressions or insights in your journal.

Reflecting and Integrating the Experience

To integrate this experience, spend a few moments each day reconnecting with the sense of peace and clarity you felt during the ritual. Practice carrying Michael's presence with you, especially in moments of doubt or uncertainty, allowing his protective strength to remind you of your place within the divine order.

Daily Reflection and Connection Each morning, take a brief moment to invite Michael's guidance as you face the day. Visualize his protective energy surrounding you, reinforcing your connection to the angelic realms and the hidden realities they govern.

Journaling Spiritual Insights and Moments of Guidance Record any signs, symbols, or moments of insight that seem connected to your ritual. Over time, you may notice patterns or messages that deepen your understanding of the spiritual realms.

Living with Awareness of the Hidden Realms Allow this ritual and its insights to transform how you see the world around you. Recognize that the physical and spiritual realms are interconnected and that your actions, thoughts, and prayers resonate beyond the material world. By honoring the divine hierarchy and maintaining a humble approach to spiritual exploration, you align yourself with the higher order Michael protects.

Embracing the Wisdom of the Angelic Realms

Understanding and connecting with the angelic realms is a journey of reverence and humility. Guided by Saint Michael, we learn that these hidden dimensions are not merely places to explore but sacred realities that reveal deeper truths about divine order. By maintaining a respectful connection to these realms, we open ourselves to the wisdom and protection they offer, enriching our spiritual journey and grounding us in a more profound understanding of the cosmos.

Recognizing the Presence of Unseen Forces: Insights from Saint Michael the Archangel

"Our Struggle Is Against Spiritual Forces": Understanding Ephesians 6:12

The words of Ephesians 6:12 reveal a powerful truth about the nature of our challenges: "For our struggle is not against flesh and blood, but against the rulers, against the authorities, against the powers of this dark world and against the spiritual forces of evil in the heavenly realms." This passage from the New Testament suggests that our greatest struggles are not physical, but spiritual, engaging unseen forces that influence our lives, beliefs, and emotions. Saint Michael, as a divine protector, is attuned to these forces, recognizing both the visible and invisible energies that shape human experience. His teachings illuminate how to discern these unseen forces, providing clarity, protection, and strength.

In Michael's view, recognizing spiritual forces goes beyond identifying darkness; it involves understanding the balance of all spiritual energies and how they interact with us. Ephesians 6:12 reveals the layers of spiritual influence that exist around us, encouraging us to see ourselves as part of a larger cosmic landscape. By becoming aware of these influences, we can actively engage with Michael's guidance to recognize and respond to them wisely.

The Talmud's Perspective on Spiritual Entities and Their Influence

In Jewish thought, the Talmud provides a layered understanding of spiritual entities. It suggests that creation is populated with beings whose roles are to influence, challenge, or protect humanity. These entities, whether angels or other spiritual forces, exist on a plane that is not fully accessible to human perception but interacts with us nonetheless. Angels like Saint Michael are depicted as messengers and protectors, while other entities act as intermediaries that bring both blessings and tests.

The Talmudic concept of these spiritual forces shows that each entity, whether benevolent or malevolent, is part of the divine order. Even forces of challenge and darkness serve a purpose, revealing humanity's need for strength, resilience, and discernment. Saint Michael's guidance emphasizes the need to discern these influences, recognizing the energies that support growth and distinguishing them from those that may hinder or mislead.

Michael's Guidance in Recognizing and Responding to Unseen Energies

Saint Michael, as a guardian of divine balance and truth, provides insight into how to recognize and respond to unseen spiritual forces. Rather than inciting fear, he encourages a balanced awareness, cultivating a sense of inner peace and protection. Through his teachings, Michael invites us to adopt a spiritual sensitivity—one that neither dismisses nor obsesses over invisible energies, but discerns them with clarity.

Michael's guidance centers on several core practices: grounding, aligning with light, and invoking protective discernment. When we encounter energies that feel unsettling or disruptive, Michael advises focusing on cultivating inner peace rather than reacting with fear or aggression. By doing so, we strengthen our natural defenses, making it more difficult for disruptive energies to take root within us. Michael also teaches that recognizing unseen forces is part of self-awareness; as we become more attuned to our inner state, we are better equipped to sense shifts in energy.

Ritual for Spiritual Discernment: Attuning to Unseen Energies with Saint Michael

This ritual is designed to help you become aware of unseen forces while maintaining a state of peace and protection under Saint Michael's guidance. The goal is not to identify every energy but to develop the discernment needed to recognize and respond to them with wisdom and strength.

Preparation: Creating a Space of Peace and Protection

Select a quiet, undisturbed area where you can create a calm and focused atmosphere. This space should be free of distractions to support your awareness of subtle energies.

Materials:

- A blue candle symbolizing Saint Michael's protective energy.
- A piece of hematite or black tourmaline to ground and anchor your energy.
- Lavender or sage incense to purify the space.
- A small bowl of saltwater for cleansing and anchoring.
- A notebook or journal to record any impressions or insights.

Setting the Space: Begin by lighting the incense and placing the blue candle in front of you. Arrange the bowl of saltwater beside the candle, with the piece of hematite or black tourmaline near it. Sit comfortably, ensuring you feel grounded and at ease.

Invocation: Calling Upon Saint Michael for Protection and Clarity

Close your eyes, take several deep breaths, and focus on centering your awareness. Feel your body relaxing and your energy settling as you prepare to connect with Saint Michael.

Say aloud:

"Saint Michael, protector and guide, I invite your presence here. Surround me with your light and clarity, helping me to recognize and understand the energies that surround me. May I be guided by discernment and strength, knowing that with your protection, I have nothing to fear."

As you speak these words, visualize a shield of light forming around you, growing brighter and stronger with each breath. Imagine this shield creating a safe boundary, through which only truth and clarity can pass.

Guided Visualization: Tuning into Subtle Energies with Michael's Guidance

With Michael's presence established, gently close your eyes and enter into a state of relaxed awareness. Visualize yourself standing in a serene field surrounded by light, with Saint Michael at your side.

1. Sensing the Presence of Energies Imagine that in this field, you can perceive various subtle energies flowing around you—some feel calm and supportive, while others may seem neutral or even slightly unsettling. Allow yourself to observe without judgment, simply noticing how each energy feels. With Michael's guidance, recognize that these forces are present and can be observed without attaching yourself to them.

2. Using the Symbol of Light for Clarity Visualize a sphere of bright, white light in front of you. Imagine that this light attracts only energies that align with your highest good, gently filtering out anything that does not serve your purpose. See this light as an extension of Michael's protection, helping you discern energies that are benevolent and true. Take a moment to observe any feelings or impressions that arise as you continue to focus on this light.

3. Recognizing Disruptive or Unsettling Forces Now, imagine Michael guiding you as you sense energies that feel disruptive or unsettling. Rather than reacting, observe these energies calmly. Recognize that they cannot harm you as long as you remain centered and aware. Michael encourages you to see these forces not as threats but as elements of the spiritual world that only have power when given attention or fear.

Take a deep breath, affirming your sense of inner peace and protection. Imagine any unsettling energies dissipating, powerless to enter your shield of light.

4. Setting an Intention of Awareness and Discernment
With Michael's guidance, set a personal intention to maintain spiritual awareness in your daily life. This intention will serve as a reminder to stay centered and aware of subtle influences around you, trusting that Michael's protection surrounds you at all times.

Silently affirm:

"With Saint Michael's guidance, I am aware of the unseen forces around me. I am grounded, protected, and discerning, recognizing all energies with peace and clarity."

Take a few moments to allow this intention to settle within you, feeling grounded in your connection to Michael's protection.

Closing the Ritual: Expression of Gratitude and Protection

When you are ready, bring your focus back to the present. Open your eyes and offer thanks to Saint Michael for his guidance and protection.

Say:

"Thank you, Saint Michael, for your guidance in helping me to discern the unseen forces around me. May I carry this awareness forward, rooted in peace, clarity, and trust."

Extinguish the blue candle, symbolizing the end of the ritual, and keep the piece of hematite or black tourmaline nearby for continued grounding.

Reflecting and Integrating the Experience

To integrate this experience, spend time each day becoming aware of your inner state, especially when you feel a shift in energy. By staying centered and grounded, you can navigate these energies with peace and clarity.

Daily Check-In on Energies Take a few moments each day to check in with your energy. Reflect on how you feel physically, mentally, and emotionally. If you notice shifts that feel unsettling, reconnect with Michael's protective presence, visualizing his light shielding you.

Grounding Practices When you feel the presence of disruptive energies, hold the piece of hematite or black tourmaline and take a few deep breaths. Visualize any negative or unsettling forces being drawn out, grounding you in stability and peace.

Journaling Moments of Awareness Record any experiences where you noticed unseen forces or subtle energy shifts. Reflect on these observations to cultivate a more refined awareness of your inner state, enhancing your discernment of spiritual energies over time.

Living with Spiritual Discernment

In learning to recognize unseen forces, we deepen our awareness of the spiritual layers around us. Guided by Saint Michael, this awareness is not rooted in fear, but in strength and clarity. By integrating these teachings into our daily lives, we develop resilience and discernment, grounded in the knowledge that we are guided and protected by higher forces of light. Through reflection, grounded practices, and a consistent connection with Saint Michael, we become more adept at navigating unseen forces with grace, maintaining peace, and aligning with our highest purpose.

Accessing Hidden Realms with Reverence and Purpose: A Journey with Saint Michael the Archangel

"Seek and You Shall Find": Understanding Matthew 7:7

In the Gospel of Matthew, the words "Seek, and you shall find; knock, and the door will be opened to you" offer a timeless encouragement for spiritual exploration. This passage conveys the importance of intent and earnestness in any quest for truth or divine understanding. For Saint Michael, this call to seek is an invitation to approach hidden realms with reverence, humility, and clear purpose. The act of seeking is not merely about curiosity but is a transformative practice that requires commitment and respect.

The phrase "seek and you shall find" resonates deeply with those who desire to approach divine mysteries. It teaches that spiritual realms and hidden truths reveal themselves not to the idle or careless, but to those who honor the journey with sincerity. Saint Michael's guidance reinforces that in these realms, one does not seek out of mere curiosity but with the profound intention to understand and connect with the divine. Michael's teachings here emphasize the respect and preparation necessary to explore these mysteries, where the journey itself is as sacred as the knowledge gained.

The Merkabah Tradition: A Pathway to the Divine Realms

In Jewish mysticism, the Merkabah tradition offers a structured, reverent approach to divine exploration, focusing on achieving states of heightened awareness that connect the seeker to spiritual realms. Named after the "chariot" (merkabah in Hebrew) seen in the prophetic visions of Ezekiel, this tradition describes a path to ascending through divine spheres to reach profound wisdom and unity with God. For the ancient mystics, these journeys required deep spiritual preparation, prayer, and meditation. The Merkabah tradition teaches that accessing divine realms must be approached with humility and purpose, for only with these qualities can one safely navigate such profound experiences.

The Merkabah tradition speaks to Saint Michael's teachings by underscoring the importance of reverence and alignment with the divine before entering these sacred spaces. As the guardian of divine order, Michael imparts that a seeker should not only seek access but also seek purification, clarity of intent, and devotion. Following these principles aligns the seeker with divine wisdom, allowing for a respectful engagement with hidden realms.

Saint Michael's Guidance on Approaching the Divine Realms

Saint Michael, as a protector and guide of spiritual wisdom, offers a clear path for approaching hidden realms with reverence and purpose. In his teachings, he emphasizes the need for a pure heart, aligned intent, and protection to navigate these spaces safely. His guidance involves a combination of preparation, invocation, and focused intention to ensure that each journey into divine realms is both respectful and insightful. Michael encourages seekers to approach with humility, as only those who truly honor the divine can gain genuine understanding.

For Michael, the journey into hidden realms is not a pursuit of power or influence but of alignment with the divine order. His teachings guide us to seek not for personal gain but for connection, insight, and the ability to serve the higher good. This orientation ensures that each step is taken with the grace and humility needed to access these realms in a way that honors their sacredness.

Ritual of Seeking: Accessing Hidden Realms under Michael's Guidance

This ritual, guided by Saint Michael, is designed to open access to hidden realms with reverence and purposeful seeking. Through this ritual, you will prepare your body, mind, and spirit, aligning with Michael's guidance to access divine realms safely and meaningfully.

Preparation: Setting Intentions and Creating a Sacred Space

Choose a time and space where you will not be interrupted, preferably a quiet, serene environment that allows you to feel both grounded and open. Ensure you are well-rested and approach this ritual with a clear and focused mind, free of distractions.

Materials:

- A blue or white candle symbolizing Saint Michael's guidance and light.

- Incense, such as frankincense or myrrh, to create a purified atmosphere.
- A small cup of saltwater to use as a cleansing and grounding element.
- A journal or notebook for recording insights and reflections.
- A symbolic key or small object representing "seeking" to hold during meditation.

Setting the Space: Arrange the candle and incense before you, placing the cup of saltwater nearby. Hold the symbolic key in your hand as a reminder of your intention to seek with humility and reverence.

Invoking Saint Michael: Opening with a Call to Guidance and Protection

Light the candle, allowing its flame to represent Michael's presence and guidance. Sit comfortably and close your eyes, taking deep breaths to center yourself.

Say aloud:

"Saint Michael, guide of divine mysteries, protector of those who seek truth with reverence, I call upon you to be my guide. Help me to approach the hidden realms with humility, wisdom, and respect. May I seek only that which aligns with the divine, and may my intentions be pure and focused on the higher good."

As you speak these words, visualize a shield of light forming around you, creating a safe boundary through which only benevolent energies may pass. Feel the presence of Michael as a calm, steady light beside you, a guardian who will walk with you through each stage of the ritual.

Guided Visualization: Journeying to the Threshold of Hidden Realms

1. Establishing a Sense of Groundedness With Michael's presence beside you, take a few moments to feel fully grounded in your body. Place your feet firmly on the ground, sensing the stability of the earth beneath you. Imagine roots growing from your feet, connecting you deeply to the earth's wisdom and strength. This groundedness is your anchor, keeping you connected to the physical realm even as you explore the spiritual.

2. Holding the Intention of Humble Seeking Hold the symbolic key in your hand, focusing on its meaning as a tool of seeking. Allow its weight to remind you of the sacred responsibility you carry in approaching hidden realms. Visualize this key as a representation of your intention to seek with a pure heart, free of ego or desire for personal gain. Silently affirm:

"I seek with reverence and purpose. I approach the divine with humility, guided by Saint Michael's wisdom."

Allow this intention to settle deeply within you, becoming the foundation of your exploration.

3. Visualization: Approaching the Threshold With Michael's light beside you, imagine yourself approaching a great door, one that marks the threshold to hidden realms. This door is beautiful, adorned with symbols that resonate with divine wisdom. Feel the weight of this moment, knowing that you stand at the edge of the unknown.

Visualize Michael standing beside you as you reach out to "knock" upon this threshold. Feel his hand on your shoulder, a reassurance that you are guided and protected in this space. Mentally affirm your readiness to seek only what aligns with divine will, allowing a deep sense of peace and surrender to fill you.

4. Receiving Insight As you knock, imagine the door slowly opening, revealing a landscape of light and subtle forms. Rather than stepping through immediately, stand on the threshold and observe. Allow any impressions, feelings, or symbols to come to you naturally. You may receive impressions of color, light, or a feeling of profound peace—these are Michael's signs of reassurance and invitation.

If a specific insight or image appears, acknowledge it with gratitude, knowing it is a part of the hidden realm's guidance for you. Allow yourself to remain in this state for as long as it feels comfortable, receiving only what aligns with the intention you set.

Setting an Intention for the Knowledge Gained

When you feel complete, step back from the threshold, closing the door mentally. Hold the key once more, affirming that you will use any insight gained only for purposes that honor the divine and support the higher good.

Say:

"I honor the wisdom received and the protection given. May any insights serve the divine order and deepen my connection to truth."

Closing the Ritual: Gratitude and Grounding

To close, thank Saint Michael for his guidance and protection.

Say:

"Thank you, Saint Michael, for guiding me with reverence and purpose. May I walk with humility and wisdom, honoring the mysteries and seeking only what aligns with the highest good."

Extinguish the candle, symbolizing the completion of this journey, and dip your fingers in the saltwater to cleanse and ground yourself. Place the symbolic key somewhere meaningful, such as an altar or sacred space, as a reminder of your intention to seek with humility.

Integrating the Experience: Reflection and Spiritual Fortification

Daily Reflection on Sacred Seeking Each day, reflect on your journey and the intention to seek with reverence. Ask yourself if your actions and choices align with this intention, helping you maintain a mindset of humility and openness.

Mindfulness of Purpose Be mindful that the insights you gained are sacred, and any actions inspired by them should reflect this respect. As you engage with others and make choices, ensure that you approach all interactions with the same reverence you brought to this ritual.

Journaling Impressions and Guidance Each evening, journal about any experiences or thoughts that resonate with the wisdom you gained from this ritual. Reflect on how these insights are influencing your actions, deepening your understanding, and helping you grow spiritually.

Walking in Reverence with Michael's Teachings

Through Saint Michael's guidance, approaching hidden realms becomes a sacred practice, grounded in respect, clarity, and humility. By seeking with purpose, you honor the divine mysteries and strengthen your connection to spiritual truth. Michael's teachings remind us that the journey itself is an act of devotion, one that transforms both the seeker and the knowledge sought. Through continued reflection, mindful actions, and the practice of humility, you deepen your alignment with these sacred realms, walking in harmony with Michael as your guide and protector.

Capstone Ritual: Embracing Saint Michael's Guidance in Hidden Realms

This Capstone Ritual serves as the culminating practice for deepening your connection with Saint Michael and opening yourself to his guidance in the hidden realms. Building on the principles and practices explored in previous rituals, this final journey emphasizes integration, introspective reflection, and alignment with Saint Michael's purpose as the protector and revealer of divine mysteries. This ritual is not about new actions but about creating a space where all prior insights coalesce into a unified, contemplative experience. The steps are condensed to allow a fluid, reflective experience, as this ritual seeks to solidify your alignment with Michael's guidance in all areas of life.

Entering the Sacred Space: Condensed Preparation for Inner Clarity

As this is the concluding ritual, the preparation is simplified to reflect the internal focus of the practice. Gather items used in prior rituals, if available, and include a unique item, like a small crystal, a feather, or a symbolic key, to signify this ritual's culminating purpose.

Materials Needed:

- A blue or white candle, representing divine light and clarity.
- Incense, such as frankincense, to purify the space.
- A cup of saltwater or a small bowl of earth for grounding.
- A symbolic item, such as a small crystal or feather, representing finality and commitment to Saint Michael's path.

Arrange these items in a familiar and sacred space. Allow your mind to settle, grounding yourself in the purpose of closure and integration.

Simple Invocation: A Call to Saint Michael's Presence

Light the candle and incense, letting their soft glow and scent establish the sacred space. Inwardly focus on your intention to enter this final stage with reverence and trust.

Say aloud:

"Saint Michael, guardian of hidden realms and divine mysteries, I seek your guidance as I open myself to the knowledge and peace of the realms unseen. May this ritual be a culmination of my journey with you, sealing my understanding and deepening my alignment with your teachings. Guide me to walk in clarity, trust, and divine purpose."

Feel his presence enveloping the space, a steady and protective light. Allow yourself to sense his strength as a reassuring force surrounding you, inviting you to rest in his guidance.

Reflective Visualization: Journeying through Hidden Realms with Michael

Guided Visualization Part I: Revisiting Your Journey
Close your eyes, taking several slow breaths as you mentally journey through the experiences of previous rituals, focusing on each theme: unity, balance, cycles, and reverence in the hidden realms. Imagine these concepts coming together as a constellation of lights within your mind, each illuminating the pathway that has led you here.

See Saint Michael standing beside you, guiding you through these recollections with understanding and compassion.

Each memory feels like a stone along a path, forming the foundation of your spiritual journey and grounding you in your growth. You sense Michael's presence as a steady force, encouraging you to trust in the wisdom you have gained.

Guided Visualization Part II: Reaching the Threshold of the Hidden Realms With Michael at your side, visualize arriving at a final door—the entryway to the hidden realms, symbolizing the place where the unknown and known unite. You stand at the threshold, aware of the journey behind and the mysteries ahead.

Michael's light surrounds you, casting an aura of calm and readiness. In your mind, allow the door to open slowly, revealing an expansive space filled with ethereal light. You do not step forward; instead, you pause, observing and feeling the energy within. This space, filled with potential and divine presence, signifies the hidden realms and the infinite wisdom they hold.

Let Michael's presence guide you to a deeper understanding of your place within this divine mystery. Take time to absorb the impressions, colors, and feelings that arise. These are not specific messages but an invitation to trust the mystery, knowing that you are supported and aligned with divine purpose.

Reflecting on the Journey: Integrating Insights and Commitments

When you feel ready, close the door in your mind, symbolizing a respectful closure to the experience. Allow yourself to return to the present space, holding onto the awareness that you carry this connection with you always.

Pick up the symbolic item—your crystal, feather, or key—and place it over your heart, affirming your commitment to continue walking in trust and reverence. Feel Michael's hand on your shoulder, a final blessing, sealing this commitment.

Say:

"I honor this journey and the guidance given by Saint Michael. May I carry forth the wisdom of the hidden realms with humility and strength. I commit to living in alignment with divine purpose, walking in faith and reverence."

Closing the Ritual: Acknowledging Saint Michael's Ongoing Guidance

To close, extinguish the candle and incense, symbolizing the end of this ritual but not the end of your connection with Saint Michael. Hold your symbolic item close to you, placing it on your altar or in a sacred space as a reminder of this journey and the insights gained.

In a whisper, say:

"Thank you, Saint Michael, for guiding me through the hidden realms and for your unending protection. May I continue to grow in alignment with the divine plan, honoring the mysteries I have encountered and the wisdom that I now carry within."

Take a moment to reflect in silence, feeling a profound sense of peace and finality as you conclude this ritual.

Integrating the Capstone Ritual into Daily Life: Living with Reverence and Purpose

This capstone ritual, though a conclusion, is also a beginning. Saint Michael's guidance remains with you, accessible through your continued actions, reflections, and spiritual practices.

Daily Practice of Reverence for the Hidden Realms Each day, take a few moments to reflect on how you can walk with reverence for the hidden realms in your everyday life.

Approach challenges and opportunities with the same mindfulness, knowing they are part of the divine mystery.

Mindful Awareness and Humility Embrace a spirit of humility, understanding that while you may not always see the larger picture, Saint Michael's guidance illuminates your path step by step. Live with trust that each experience, whether clear or obscured, has its place in your spiritual growth.

Regular Meditation for Continued Alignment Set aside time weekly for silent meditation with Saint Michael, allowing his presence to renew your alignment with his teachings. This quiet time serves as a reminder that, while the ritual may be complete, the connection to Michael and the hidden realms endures.

Through this Capstone Ritual, you step into a life of continuous exploration, guided by Saint Michael's wisdom, strength, and protection. Embrace the mystery of the hidden realms with trust, and know that every step forward strengthens your alignment with the divine.

As we transition from exploring the hidden realms to understanding the metaphysical principles governing the universe, we begin to look at the foundational laws that uphold cosmic order and interconnection. In this section, Saint Michael guides us deeper into the universal principles that shape existence, such as the Law of Balance and Harmony, Cause and Effect, and the Interdependence of All Beings and Forces. These principles reveal the unseen architecture supporting both the spiritual and physical worlds, helping us understand how each action, thought, and relationship influences the whole. With insights drawn from scripture and Kabbalistic teachings, we delve into how Saint Michael's role as a guardian of divine justice is interwoven with these universal laws. This next chapter invites us to harmonize our lives with these cosmic principles, offering meditation practices to internalize and reflect upon these truths in our daily walk with Saint Michael's wisdom.

5. The Universal Laws: Saint Michael's Guide to Metaphysical Principles Governing Creation

As we journey into the heart of metaphysical principles, Saint Michael invites us to explore the universal laws that serve as the foundation for all existence. These laws—Balance and Harmony, Cause and Effect, and the Interdependence of All Beings and Forces—reveal the intricate design of creation, where each force, action, and soul plays an essential role. Rooted in ancient wisdom from Proverbs, Job, and the Zohar, and drawing upon Saint Michael's guidance, we uncover how these laws manifest both in the heavens and within our own lives. Through the Law of Balance, we understand the necessity of justice and harmony, upheld by Michael's role as a cosmic guardian. With the Principle of Cause and Effect, we learn how each choice creates a ripple in the spiritual and physical realms, teaching us to act with greater awareness and purpose. Finally, through the Interdependence of All, we glimpse the unity that binds every being in a sacred web of existence. Together, these principles encourage us to live in harmony with the divine design, and in alignment with Saint Michael's teachings. This chapter includes meditation practices to help us embody and reflect upon these cosmic laws, deepening our connection to the universal order and our role within it.

The Law of Balance and Harmony: Saint Michael's Path to Cosmic Equilibrium

The concept of balance is woven through the universe, holding creation together in a harmonious flow. In this exploration, we examine how Saint Michael, as a cosmic guardian, upholds the Law of Balance and Harmony, acting as a mediator between justice and mercy, light and shadow, peace and power. Guided by the timeless wisdom of *Proverbs* and the mystical teachings of the *Kabbalah*, we explore balance as both a metaphysical principle and a living force that sustains life itself.

"A Just Balance is God's Delight" – The Wisdom of Proverbs

The Bible in *Proverbs 11:1* states:

"A just balance is God's delight."

This verse captures the divine essence of balance. Unlike the notion of rigid justice, balance implies a responsive, adaptive approach to justice that maintains harmony within the diversity of creation. A "just balance" speaks to the delicate interplay of cosmic forces, suggesting that equilibrium is not static but a living, dynamic state. In this context, Saint Michael embodies a "living justice," where he does not impose harsh rigidity but instead ensures fairness and adaptability, allowing the natural flow of creation to maintain balance.

Through this role, Michael teaches that balance within the universe is not merely about equality but about each element being exactly where it needs to be—aligned with divine will. In essence, balance is the core of harmony and the foundation of creation.

Kabbalistic Insights on Balance: Interplay of Divine Forces

In *Kabbalah*, the concept of balance is central to the structure of the cosmos. The *Tree of Life*, a foundational symbol in Kabbalistic mysticism, illustrates the balance between opposing forces, known as *Chesed* (kindness) and

Gevurah (severity or judgment). These forces exist on either side of the Tree, with *Tiferet*—representing harmony or beauty—at the center to balance them. This layout reflects a cosmic truth: harmony arises not from eliminating contrast but from balancing it.

For Saint Michael, who navigates the realms of mercy and judgment, the Kabbalistic Tree of Life becomes a practical map for upholding balance. Michael's guidance in this tradition is not to erase or overcome opposition but to mediate, allowing both mercy and justice to coexist, revealing harmony as the divine goal. Through Michael's teachings, we understand that spiritual balance involves accepting opposites and finding unity within them.

Saint Michael's Role in Upholding Cosmic Balance

Saint Michael's role extends far beyond that of a warrior; he acts as a universal mediator who ensures equilibrium across divine realms. By sustaining balance between forces of light and shadow, order and transformation, Michael enables all beings to fulfill their roles without collapsing into chaos. His guidance encourages us to seek balance within ourselves, to live aligned with the universe's natural harmony.

Michael's guardianship over balance is especially relevant when we confront personal or spiritual conflicts. Just as he maintains the cosmic equilibrium, he offers us the strength and wisdom to approach challenges without extremes. In this way, Michael acts as a divine "scale" upon which all things are weighed, urging us to approach life's trials with a balanced heart and mind.

Ritual for Invoking Balance and Harmony Through Saint Michael's Guidance

This ritual is designed to help you experience and embody the Law of Balance and Harmony, with Saint Michael as your guide. Each step is crafted to align your inner energy with the divine equilibrium present throughout creation. By following this practice, you invite Michael's wisdom into your life, reinforcing the sense of balance in your actions, thoughts, and spiritual journey.

Preparation: Setting the Space for Balance

Choose a serene space for this ritual, ideally where you can incorporate natural elements. Begin by gathering these items:

- **A pair of scales or balanced stones** to represent harmony
- **Two candles**: one white (for clarity and peace) and one blue (for divine protection and balance)
- **Incense** such as sandalwood or lavender, to create a calming atmosphere
- **A small bowl of water and a handful of salt**, symbolizing purification and grounding
- **A notebook or journal** to record reflections

Step 1: Centering and Invocation of Saint Michael

To begin, light the incense, letting the scent fill your space. As you prepare yourself, imagine a gentle, encompassing light forming around you, a sphere of peace and calm.

Then, place your hand over your heart and say aloud:

"Saint Michael, protector and mediator of divine balance, I invite your presence into this space. Guide me toward harmony within myself and with all creation. Help me embody your wisdom, so I may walk in balance and serve as a vessel of peace and justice in the world."

Take a moment to feel Michael's presence, a steadying and protective energy that surrounds and centers you.

Step 2: Reflecting on Proverbs 11:1

Read *Proverbs 11:1* aloud:

"A just balance is God's delight."

Allow these words to resonate, imagining how balance permeates all creation, from the stars to the smallest particles. Visualize Michael as a steadying force, maintaining this balance in both the seen and unseen realms.

Consider how these words apply to your life. In what areas might you invite more balance? Where could you bring harmony between mercy and judgment, action and reflection? Allow these insights to rise naturally, observing them without judgment.

Step 3: Aligning with the Elements of Balance

Light the white and blue candles, representing harmony and divine protection. Place the balanced stones or scales in front of you, contemplating their symbolic weight. Then, sprinkle the salt into the bowl of water, watching as the two merge seamlessly.

Hold your hands over the bowl and say:

"As salt and water come together in balance, may my spirit align with the divine equilibrium. Saint Michael, guide me toward harmony in thought, word, and deed."

This action reinforces the concept that balance is achieved through unity, blending distinct aspects of ourselves into a cohesive whole.

Step 4: Visualizing Balance Within and Around You

Close your eyes and visualize yourself standing in a peaceful, illuminated space. In this space, see a pair of scales suspended before you. One side holds your strengths, your light, and the qualities you are proud of. The other holds your shadows, fears, or challenges. Visualize these scales, noticing any imbalance between them.

Invite Saint Michael to stand beside you, his hand gently steadying the scales. Allow his energy to flow into both sides, balancing them. Feel the weight of both your light and shadow, accepting each as a vital part of your being.

Say aloud:

"Saint Michael, guardian of balance, may I accept both light and shadow within me. Help me carry each with grace and humility, trusting in your guidance to walk the path of harmony."

Allow this balance to settle within you, a quiet but profound equilibrium.

Step 5: Setting an Intention for Balance in Your Life

With your hands over your heart, set an intention to carry this sense of balance forward in your life. Speak this intention aloud:

"I am in harmony with all that I am. I honor my strengths and embrace my shadows, knowing each has its purpose. Guided by Saint Michael, I will walk the path of balance and live in alignment with the divine harmony of creation."

Feel this intention grounding within you, a quiet commitment to pursue balance with awareness and compassion.

Step 6: Closing and Integrating Balance

To close the ritual, extinguish the candles, symbolizing the integration of balance into your life. Thank Saint Michael for his presence and guidance, bowing your head in gratitude.

Place the scales or stones in a special location as a reminder of this commitment to balance.

Take a moment to breathe deeply, allowing the energy of the ritual to settle within you. As you complete this ritual, feel the quiet assurance that you are aligned with the cosmic balance that Michael upholds.

Integrating the Law of Balance and Harmony in Daily Life

After performing the ritual, continue to embody Saint Michael's teachings on balance and harmony in your everyday actions. Small, mindful practices can reinforce this sense of equilibrium, fostering a steady, resilient spirit.

Morning Reflection: Setting an Intention for Balance

Each morning, take a moment to set an intention to carry balance into your day. Visualize Michael's presence, guiding you to approach each interaction and choice with a harmonious mind. This reflection aligns you with Michael's wisdom and prepares you to face the day with composure.

Observing Balance in Your Surroundings

Throughout the day, take moments to observe balance within nature or your environment. Notice the harmony in trees, animals, or the flow of a river. By observing balance externally, you reinforce your internal harmony, grounding yourself in the natural rhythm of life.

Journaling: Reflection on Balance and Harmony

In the evening, consider keeping a journal where you reflect on how balance appeared in your day. Note any situations where you felt in harmony—or out of it—and how you responded. Reflect on how you might approach similar situations with greater balance tomorrow, integrating Michael's teachings into your thoughts and actions.

Embodying Divine Balance: Living in Alignment with Saint Michael's Wisdom

By understanding and practicing the Law of Balance and Harmony, you align yourself with the natural flow of the universe, living as a vessel of divine equilibrium. Saint Michael's guidance teaches that balance is not about avoiding conflict or challenges but embracing each part of life with awareness, compassion, and acceptance. Through small, mindful actions and the insights gained from this ritual, you cultivate a life grounded in peace, clarity, and purpose—qualities that enable you to serve as a beacon of balance for yourself and others.

The Principle of Cause and Effect: Saint Michael's Teachings on Actions and Their Spiritual Consequences

At the heart of spiritual practice lies a universal truth: every action carries a ripple, a consequence that flows through the fabric of creation. Known as the Principle of Cause and Effect, this metaphysical law operates as a guiding force in the universe, shaping experiences and outcomes according to the seeds we sow. Saint Michael, with his role as a guardian of divine justice, exemplifies this principle, guiding souls to act with intention and to understand the profound impact of their actions.

"Those Who Sow Trouble Reap It" – Wisdom from the Book of Job

In *Job 4:8*, we read:

"Those who sow trouble reap it."

This verse from *Job* is a powerful statement on the spiritual and ethical implications of our actions. Within this wisdom is the teaching that every deed is a seed planted in the soil of existence, one that will inevitably bear fruit, for better or worse. When we act with malice or selfish intent, we plant seeds that grow into difficulties or obstacles, not only affecting others but returning to shape our own lives. In this light, Saint Michael's teachings encourage us to act with awareness, reminding us that the path we create for others ultimately becomes our own.

For Saint Michael, who upholds divine justice, understanding cause and effect is essential to the spiritual path. As an archangel, he safeguards the moral order of the universe, ensuring that actions aligned with truth and kindness are rewarded, while those driven by harm or deceit are met with consequence. Through Michael's guidance, we are invited to consider the true impact of our choices, learning to cultivate deeds that serve the greater harmony of all beings.

Jewish Teachings on Cause and Effect: Insights from Pirkei Avot

The *Pirkei Avot*, or "Ethics of the Fathers," offers timeless insights into the law of cause and effect, emphasizing that every action is interwoven into a chain of consequences. One of the most famous teachings is from *Pirkei Avot 2:1*, where Rabbi Yehudah HaNasi states:

"Consider the consequences of your actions."

This teaching reinforces the idea that actions should not be viewed in isolation but as part of an ongoing sequence that shapes both individual lives and the collective human experience. Cause and effect is seen as a continuous cycle that unfolds in complex patterns, leading to growth, decay, harmony, or disruption depending on the quality of one's actions.

In alignment with this teaching, Saint Michael encourages a holistic approach to decision-making, one that acknowledges the interconnectedness of all beings. Acting with reverence for cause and effect means choosing thoughts, words, and deeds that contribute to positive outcomes not only for oneself but for the broader world. Michael's guidance in this context is one of mindfulness and compassion, empowering us to honor the sacred responsibility we have toward one another and to the universe itself.

Saint Michael's Teachings on Spiritual Consequences: Sowing Seeds of Harmony and Integrity

As a guardian of divine justice, Saint Michael embodies the spiritual principle that each action we take is a seed with the potential to grow into either harmony or discord. His teachings remind us that by sowing seeds of integrity, kindness, and courage, we contribute to a world of balance and peace. Conversely, acts of malice or neglect do not simply disappear but continue to impact the spiritual environment, creating ripples that must eventually return to us.

Michael's role in this cosmic process is not to judge but to guide and protect. He stands as a symbol of accountability, reminding us that the universe is alive with cause and effect, that nothing goes unnoticed, and that every action shapes the future. Through his teachings, we learn that spiritual integrity requires us to be conscious cultivators, to plant seeds of kindness, courage, and truth, knowing that these qualities not only uplift others but also build a foundation of strength and resilience within ourselves.

Ritual for Honoring Cause and Effect with Saint Michael's Guidance

This ritual is designed to help you connect deeply with the principle of cause and effect, encouraging you to reflect on past actions and set intentions for sowing seeds of harmony and positive change. Guided by Saint Michael, this practice fosters an awareness of the ripples your actions create, helping you cultivate an approach to life that honors integrity, responsibility, and spiritual awareness.

Preparation: Gathering Symbols of Cause and Effect

Begin by choosing a peaceful space, ideally one that allows for undisturbed contemplation. Gather the following items:

- **A seed or small plant**, symbolizing the actions we plant in life
- **A white candle**, representing clarity and purity of intention
- **A small mirror** to reflect on past actions
- **Incense** such as frankincense or sandalwood, to purify and create a sacred atmosphere
- **A notebook or journal** for recording reflections and intentions

Step 1: Centering and Invocation of Saint Michael

Light the incense and let its scent fill the space, setting the tone for introspection and spiritual awareness. Light the candle and place it before you, focusing on its steady flame as a symbol of clarity and wisdom.

With your hand over your heart, say aloud:

"Saint Michael, guardian of divine justice, I invite your presence here. Guide me in understanding the power of my actions, the seeds I sow, and the ripples I create. Help me to act with intention, awareness, and compassion, sowing only that which uplifts and harmonizes."

Take a few deep breaths, feeling Saint Michael's protective energy surrounding you, bringing a sense of accountability and peace.

Step 2: Reflection on Job 4:8

Read *Job 4:8* aloud:

"Those who sow trouble reap it."

Allow these words to resonate, reflecting on times when you may have sown seeds of kindness, courage, or wisdom—and moments where perhaps actions were taken out of fear, anger, or impulse. Recognize that each of these choices has contributed to the person you are today and to the world around you.

Consider how you might consciously sow seeds that reflect your highest intentions, actions that contribute to harmony and growth for yourself and others.

Step 3: Mirror Reflection: Gaining Clarity on Past Actions

Hold the mirror before you and gaze into it, using it as a symbolic tool to look within. Reflect on recent choices or actions that have impacted your life and others, both positively and negatively.

Say aloud:

"Saint Michael, help me to see the seeds I have sown clearly, to understand the paths I have created. May I look upon my actions with honesty and learn from them, guided by your wisdom."

As you look into the mirror, allow insights to arise naturally, without judgment. See this reflection as an opportunity to learn, to recognize patterns, and to commit to sowing seeds of kindness, courage, and compassion going forward.

Step 4: Planting the Seed: Setting Intentions for Future Actions

Hold the seed or small plant in your hands, feeling its potential for growth. Imagine it as a representation of the actions you will take, the choices you will make, and the ripples you will create.

Plant the seed or place the plant in a small pot of soil. As you do so, say:

"With Saint Michael's guidance, I plant this seed as a symbol of my commitment to act with integrity, compassion, and mindfulness. May each choice I make serve the highest good, creating ripples of harmony and growth."

Feel this action grounding your intentions, a tangible reminder of the principle of cause and effect. Recognize that, like this seed, your actions will grow and bear fruit according to the energy you put into them.

Step 5: Setting an Intention for Mindful Action

With your hands over your heart, set a personal intention to approach future actions with awareness of their spiritual consequences. Speak this intention aloud:

"I am mindful of the seeds I sow, knowing that each action creates ripples that shape my life and the lives of others. May I act with kindness, courage, and wisdom, guided by Saint Michael, upholding the harmony of creation."

Feel this intention resonate within, grounding it as a commitment to walk a path of integrity.

Step 6: Closing and Integrating the Ritual

To close, extinguish the candle as a symbol of bringing your insights into the inner world. Thank Saint Michael for his guidance and presence, bowing your head in gratitude.

Take a few moments to center yourself, feeling the wisdom of cause and effect settle into your spirit. Keep the seed or plant in a visible place, serving as a reminder of your commitment to act with intention and awareness.

Integrating the Principle of Cause and Effect into Daily Life

After completing the ritual, continue embodying Saint Michael's teachings on cause and effect by practicing intentionality and mindfulness in your actions, words, and thoughts.

Morning Reflection: Setting an Intention for Mindful Choices

Each morning, take a moment to reflect on the potential of the day ahead. Set a simple intention to act with kindness and integrity, visualizing Saint Michael's presence guiding you toward choices that align with your highest values.

Observing the Ripples of Your Actions

Throughout the day, observe how your actions, no matter how small, create ripples. Whether through a kind word, a helpful gesture, or a moment of patience, recognize that each act carries energy that affects others. This practice reinforces your connection to the principle of cause and effect, helping you make choices that uplift and harmonize.

Evening Reflection: Reflecting on the Day's Actions

In the evening, consider keeping a journal where you reflect on the day's choices and their effects. Note moments where your actions contributed to harmony or any instances where there may have been discord. Reflect on how you might approach similar situations tomorrow, bringing a deeper understanding of cause and effect into your daily life.

Embracing the Power of Intention: Walking in Alignment with Saint Michael's Teachings

By honoring the Principle of Cause and Effect, you align with the natural order of the universe, understanding that each action, word, and thought contributes to the greater fabric of existence. Through Saint Michael's guidance, you become a conscious cultivator, sowing seeds that bring peace, compassion, and strength into the world. As you walk this path, you embody Michael's teachings, creating ripples that not only enrich your life but also contribute to the harmony of all creation.

The Interdependence of All Beings and Forces: Saint Michael's Teachings on Unity in Diversity

As we explore the metaphysical principles that govern the universe, we arrive at a profound truth: all beings and forces are interconnected, bound together in a divine tapestry that shapes and sustains existence. This principle of interdependence is more than a philosophical idea—it is a lived reality, deeply woven into the fabric of creation and the heart of Saint Michael's teachings. Through scripture, mystic texts, and Saint Michael's insights, we can come to understand this unity in diversity, seeing ourselves as participants in a cosmic web of shared purpose and destiny.

"Unity in Diversity" – The Apostle Paul's Message in 1 Corinthians 12:12-27

In *1 Corinthians 12:12-27*, the Apostle Paul presents a powerful metaphor to illustrate the interdependence of all beings, likening each part of creation to the body of Christ:

"For just as the body is one and has many members, and all the members of the body, though many, are one body, so it is with Christ... The eye cannot say to the hand, 'I have no need of you,' nor again the head to the feet, 'I have no need of you.' On the contrary, the parts of the body that seem to be weaker are indispensable."

Paul's message reminds us that while each part of creation holds a unique function, every individual part contributes to a unified whole. This concept of unity in diversity serves as a foundation for understanding our spiritual interconnectedness. Like organs in a body, we each have a role that, while distinct, is essential to the greater harmony.

For Saint Michael, this interconnectedness is sacred, not only in the material realm but also in the spiritual. Every being, every soul, every element of creation works in concert, influencing and supporting one another. Just as the Apostle Paul illustrates, there is no being or force that exists in isolation. To ignore this unity is to ignore the essence of divine creation. By recognizing the sanctity of interconnectedness, we step closer to fulfilling our purpose within the divine plan.

Zoharic Wisdom on Divine Interdependence: The Cosmic Tree of Life

The *Zohar*, a cornerstone of Jewish mysticism, delves deeply into the concept of interdependence within the structure of the *Tree of Life*, a symbolic diagram that maps the flow of divine energy throughout creation. Each sphere, or *sefirah*, on the Tree represents a different attribute of God and is interconnected with others, allowing divine energy to flow through each channel harmoniously.

In the *Zohar*, these spheres are not isolated aspects of divinity but work together to create a balanced and functioning whole. For instance, *Chesed* (loving-kindness) and *Gevurah* (strength or judgment) are interdependent, each one balancing the other to create harmony. This concept extends beyond the divine attributes to every aspect of creation. In essence, each part of the cosmos is like a branch on this tree, dependent on the rest for sustenance, structure, and purpose.

For those following Saint Michael's teachings, the *Tree of Life* serves as a map for understanding interdependence on both a personal and cosmic level. Michael's role as a guardian of divine harmony echoes the balance and unity represented in the Tree. By embracing this interdependence, we align with the divine flow of creation, moving in harmony with the forces that govern the universe. Recognizing ourselves as both individuals and parts of the greater whole brings peace, humility, and clarity to our spiritual journeys.

Insights from Saint Michael on Interconnectedness and Spiritual Unity

As a divine protector, Saint Michael embodies the unity and interconnectedness of all beings. His insights offer us a roadmap for living with a deep awareness of our spiritual ties to one another. To Saint Michael, each thought, action, and intention resonates through the web of creation, influencing not only ourselves but also the broader cosmic order. His teachings encourage us to cultivate relationships rooted in mutual respect and compassion, understanding that our lives are threads in a much larger fabric.

Michael's guidance teaches that unity in diversity does not mean sameness. Each soul, like each aspect of creation, has a unique role that contributes to the symphony of existence. By honoring these roles and recognizing the sacredness of interdependence, we foster a spiritual unity that uplifts all beings. Michael calls upon us to act in ways that strengthen these connections, to see our lives not in isolation but as part of a continuous exchange of energy, support, and purpose.

Ritual of Interconnection: Aligning with the Divine Web of Unity

This ritual, guided by Saint Michael's teachings, is designed to help you experience and honor your connection to the vast web of interdependence within creation. By aligning your spirit with the principle of interconnectedness, you will deepen your awareness of the shared destiny and purpose that links all beings.

Preparation: Gathering Sacred Symbols of Unity

To honor the theme of interconnectedness, gather the following items:

- **A small web-like item**, such as a piece of lace or a spider's web-inspired charm, symbolizing the divine web of interdependence.
- **A candle** in a color that resonates with unity, such as deep blue or white, representing spiritual connection.
- **Incense**, such as frankincense or sandalwood, to create a sacred atmosphere and invite reflection.
- **A small mirror**, to reflect on your place within the interconnected web.
- **Notebook or journal** for insights and reflections.

Step 1: Centering and Invocation of Saint Michael

Light the incense, allowing the scent to create a sense of sacred space. Sit comfortably and place the candle before you, lighting it as a symbol of spiritual unity.

With your hand over your heart, say:

"Saint Michael, guardian of divine harmony, I invite your presence here. Help me to recognize my place within the sacred web of creation, to honor the divine unity that binds us all. May I act with compassion, awareness, and gratitude for the interdependence of all beings."

Feel Michael's protective energy enveloping you, bringing a sense of peace and unity.

Step 2: Reflection on 1 Corinthians 12:12-27

Read the passage from *1 Corinthians 12:12-27* aloud:

"For just as the body is one and has many members, and all the members of the body, though many, are one body…"

Reflect on these words, contemplating how your unique strengths and experiences contribute to the whole. Consider the roles you play in the lives of others, and how your actions influence the greater spiritual ecosystem. See yourself as an essential, valued part of this "body" of creation.

Step 3: Mirror Reflection – Seeing Yourself in the Web of Life

Hold the mirror in front of you and gaze into it, using it as a symbolic tool to reflect on your place in the divine web. Imagine that the mirror reflects not only your own image but the faces, spirits, and energies of those you are connected with. Visualize the web of relationships, roles, and purposes that link you to others, each thread representing an interaction, a shared purpose, or a spiritual lesson.

Say aloud:

"Saint Michael, help me to see myself as part of the divine web. May I honor my connections, understanding that every thought, action, and word contributes to the balance of creation."

Allow yourself to feel the sacredness of these connections and to recognize the beauty of your place within the interconnected whole.

Step 4: Symbolic Offering – Honoring Interdependence

Take the web-like item, holding it in both hands as a symbol of the unity and diversity in the universe. Close your eyes, and in your mind, offer gratitude for each person, spirit, and force that has shaped your journey. Speak these words aloud:

"With Saint Michael's guidance, I honor the web of life, the divine unity that connects us all. I offer gratitude for each being, each force that weaves together the sacred tapestry of existence. May I act with respect, compassion, and awareness of my place in this greater whole."

Visualize this gratitude radiating outward, touching each part of the web and infusing it with light.

Step 5: Setting an Intention for Unity in Daily Life

Place your hands over your heart, focusing on a commitment to honor interdependence in your thoughts, words, and actions. Speak this intention aloud:

"I am one with all creation. Guided by Saint Michael, I commit to nurturing connections that uplift, support, and sustain the sacred web of life. May I recognize my role and honor the unity that binds us all."

Feel this intention taking root within you, solidifying as a guiding principle in your daily life.

Step 6: Closing and Integrating the Ritual

To close, thank Saint Michael for his guidance, bowing your head in gratitude. Extinguish the candle as a symbol of the light you carry within, a light that contributes to the greater illumination of creation.

Take a few moments to center yourself, feeling the sense of interconnectedness that the ritual has fostered. Keep the web-like item in a visible place as a reminder of the sacred unity you share with all beings.

Integrating the Principle of Interdependence into Daily Life

After the ritual, embrace Saint Michael's teachings on interconnectedness by incorporating mindful practices that honor unity and interdependence in your daily life.

Morning Meditation on Unity

Begin each morning with a brief meditation, visualizing yourself as part of a vast, interconnected web. Feel gratitude for the connections in your life and set an intention to approach each interaction with respect and awareness of this unity.

Act with Compassion and Awareness

Throughout the day, remember that every action, word, and thought influences others and contributes to the larger tapestry of creation. Approach your actions with compassion, considering how you can uplift and support those around you.

Reflective Journaling on Interdependence

Each evening, reflect on moments when you felt connected to others or aware of the greater whole. Record insights and lessons from these experiences, observing how they shape your understanding of interdependence. This practice will reinforce your awareness of interconnectedness and deepen your alignment with Saint Michael's teachings.

Embracing Interconnectedness as a Path to Divine Fulfillment

Living in alignment with Saint Michael's teachings on interdependence means recognizing that we are part of something infinitely greater than ourselves. By embodying unity in diversity, we become conscious participants in the divine harmony that sustains all existence. As we honor this sacred web, we walk in step with Saint Michael, bringing peace, balance, and purpose to our lives and to the world around us.

Meditation Practice for Integrating Metaphysical Principles Governing the Universe

This meditation practice is designed to deepen your alignment with the metaphysical principles of the universe as taught by Saint Michael, focusing on the interconnectedness of balance, cause and effect, and the unity of all beings. Through this meditation, you will tune into these cosmic laws, allowing their wisdom to resonate within you and guide your daily actions.

Preparation: Creating a Sacred Space

Before beginning, find a quiet and comfortable place where you will not be disturbed. Gather items that represent each principle you have explored:

- **A balance scale** or an image of scales for the Law of Balance and Harmony
- **A seed or small stone** to symbolize the Principle of Cause and Effect, representing growth from a single action
- **A small mirror** or crystal to reflect the interdependence and unity of all beings and forces

Arrange these items around you, with a candle at the center to symbolize divine illumination. Light the candle, and, if desired, light incense to purify the space.

Invocation
Sit comfortably, close your eyes, and place your hands over your heart. Take a few deep breaths, centering your mind. Then, invite Saint Michael's guidance with the following words:

"Saint Michael, guardian of divine balance and unity, I call upon your presence. Help me align with the principles that govern the universe, to honor balance, recognize the impact of my actions, and see myself as part of the divine unity of all creation. Guide me in integrating these cosmic truths into my heart and my life."

The Meditation Practice: Three Stages of Cosmic Integration

Each stage of this meditation is dedicated to one of the metaphysical principles. Move slowly and intentionally through each part, pausing to internalize the teachings of each principle.

Stage One: Aligning with the Law of Balance and Harmony

As you begin, bring to mind the concept of balance and harmony. Imagine a set of scales before you, each side perfectly balanced. Visualize your life as part of this cosmic balance, with every action, thought, and emotion contributing to an overall harmony.

Reflect on moments in your life where you sought balance, or where imbalance taught you valuable lessons. Acknowledge that balance is an ongoing process, a dance between giving and receiving, action and rest.

In your mind, repeat:

"Divine harmony flows through me. I am in balance with myself, others, and creation. With Saint Michael's guidance, I honor the law of balance and seek harmony in all that I do."

Spend a few moments allowing this feeling of balance to fill you, envisioning a harmonious light around you that connects you to the universe.

Stage Two: Embracing the Principle of Cause and Effect

Now, turn your attention to the Principle of Cause and Effect. Imagine holding a seed in your hand—a symbol of potential and consequence. Picture yourself planting this seed in the earth, watching as it grows, blossoms, and impacts the surrounding environment.

Think of past actions, both positive and challenging, and the outcomes they have created in your life. Acknowledge that every thought and choice sends ripples through the web of life, impacting yourself and others.

In your mind, repeat:

"Every action has meaning. Guided by Saint Michael, I choose wisely and act with purpose, knowing that my thoughts, words, and deeds shape my world."

Feel the responsibility and empowerment of this principle, committing to sow seeds of kindness, compassion, and integrity.

Stage Three: Uniting with the Interdependence of All Beings and Forces

In this final stage, focus on the unity and interdependence of all beings. Picture yourself standing within a vast web of light, each strand connecting to others, representing the lives, energies, and spirits around you.

Sense the presence of countless others—humans, animals, plants, celestial beings—who are all interconnected in divine unity. Feel Saint Michael's protective energy embracing the entire web, preserving its balance.

In your mind, repeat:

"I am one with all beings. With Saint Michael's guidance, I honor the unity that connects us all. May I act with respect, compassion, and awareness of my place in the divine web."

Allow yourself to fully experience this unity, feeling your heart expand with empathy and a sense of shared purpose.

Closing the Meditation

As you conclude, bring your awareness back to your breathing. Place your hands over your heart once more, feeling the integration of these cosmic principles within you. Open your eyes, allowing yourself a few moments to adjust and reflect on the experience.

To close, extinguish the candle, symbolizing the internalization of these truths. Offer gratitude to Saint Michael for his guidance with the words:

"Thank you, Saint Michael, for revealing the sacred principles that guide the universe. May I live with balance, mindfulness, and compassion, honoring the unity of all beings and the impact of my every choice."

Post-Meditation Reflection and Integration Practices

To reinforce the meditation's teachings, practice the following reflections and daily actions that align with the principles of balance, cause and effect, and interdependence.

Daily Reflection on Balance

Each morning, reflect on how you can bring balance into your day. Ask yourself where harmony is needed—whether in relationships, work, or personal habits—and set an intention to cultivate it. In moments of stress or conflict, visualize the scales of balance, reminding yourself to seek a middle ground.

Mindful Actions and Cause and Effect

Before making significant decisions, pause to consider the potential consequences of your actions. Ask yourself, "What seeds am I planting?" By remaining mindful of cause and effect, you strengthen your ability to choose actions that benefit both yourself and others.

In the evening, journal briefly on the choices you made and their outcomes. Reflect on how even small actions contribute to larger patterns in your life.

Embracing Unity in Relationships

Throughout your day, cultivate a sense of unity by practicing compassion and respect in your interactions. When engaging with others, remind yourself that you are part of a larger whole, and your words and actions influence the harmony of that whole.

Each week, take a few moments to reflect on connections you've made or strengthened. Recognize the value of those relationships and the shared growth that results from honoring interdependence.

Living in Alignment with Saint Michael's Teachings

By incorporating these reflections and practices, you align yourself with the metaphysical principles that govern the universe. With Saint Michael as your guide, these truths will become part of your spiritual foundation, enriching your journey with balance, intentionality, and unity. As you continue to honor these principles, you will walk with greater harmony and purpose, embodying the cosmic wisdom that sustains all creation.

As we move deeper into the teachings of Saint Michael, we enter a realm where divine purpose meets practical application through the power of magic. In this section, "Magic from Saint Michael's Perspective," we explore how Saint Michael's wisdom translates into protective, transformative, and truth-seeking practices that elevate and empower our spiritual journey. Through sacred texts and the rich traditions of both Christian and Jewish mysticism, Saint Michael's guidance helps us harness divine protection, purify energies, and foster discernment in the face of challenges. We'll also delve into balancing and banishment rituals, aligning with the elements, consecrating tools, and invoking Saint Michael's presence, revealing the depth and discipline required to wield these magics with reverence. Here, Saint Michael serves as a guide not only to understanding the principles behind each magical practice but to living in alignment with the divine light that sustains and empowers them.

6. Empowered by Divine Light: Practical Magic Through the Guidance of Saint Michael

In this section, Empowered by Divine Light, we delve into the transformative and protective aspects of magic as illuminated by Saint Michael's wisdom. Guided by his role as a defender of truth, purifier of energies, and wielder of divine light, we explore practices designed to shield, transform, discern, and sanctify. Each topic opens a door to practical magic that supports our spiritual integrity and enhances our connection to the divine forces at work in the universe. Through sacred scriptures and teachings from Christian and Jewish mystical traditions, we'll learn how Saint Michael empowers us to shield ourselves and our surroundings, cleanse negativity, discern truth with clarity, and sanctify our spiritual tools. This journey culminates with a ritual invocation to invite Saint Michael's protective presence and guidance, equipping us with the knowledge and practices to walk forward with courage, resilience, and profound spiritual alignment. Here, we invite not only the power of Saint Michael's protection but also the light of discernment and purification into our magical work, enabling us to approach each aspect of life with heightened purpose and divine insight.

Divine Protection and Shielding Magic: Saint Michael's Blueprint for Spiritual Defense

Protection and shielding magic lie at the heart of Saint Michael's teachings, reflecting his role as a guardian and warrior of divine justice. As we navigate spiritual practice and life's unseen realms, invoking Saint Michael's guidance offers us a powerful layer of spiritual security, illuminating ways to fortify ourselves against negativity, chaos, and unwanted influences. Rooted in sacred scriptures, Jewish protective traditions, and the profound shield of Saint

Michael's light, this practice offers us tools to ground our well-being in divine assurance and resilience.

"He Will Command His Angels Concerning You": Protection in Psalm 91

Psalm 91 is often called the *Psalm of Protection*, echoing the promise of divine safeguarding against forces that could harm or mislead. The verse, "He will command his angels concerning you to guard you in all your ways" (Psalm 91:11), embodies the assurance that those in alignment with the divine receive angelic protection on their path. This verse underscores Saint Michael's role as an angelic protector who brings his light and power to guard those who call upon him.

Through this psalm, Saint Michael's presence becomes a conduit of divine will, as he and other angels are summoned to offer a powerful shield for those who seek it with a sincere heart. When reciting or reflecting on this psalm, one is encouraged to visualize the protective light of Saint Michael encircling them, providing both physical and spiritual security, strengthening our resilience against worldly and unseen adversities.

Shielding Magic in Jewish Tradition: Protective Prayers and Charms

Jewish mysticism has long embraced prayers and charms for protection, grounded in the belief that divine words and symbols can repel harmful forces. Protective prayers, known as *tefillot*, as well as amulets and inscriptions, have been traditional means to summon the guardianship of angels. In Hebrew lore, invoking the names of angels, especially Michael, can bring about protection from hostile energies. The names of archangels are often inscribed on charms, invoking their unique powers to ward off negativity and provide spiritual fortification.

Saint Michael, being associated with strength, justice, and defense, is often called upon as a frontline protector. His name, which means "Who is like God?" serves as a reminder that his power is derived from divine alignment and unity with the Creator. This tradition highlights how wearing charms with Michael's name or keeping his likeness nearby symbolizes both his presence and the shield he offers.

Saint Michael's Light as a Shield: Practical Steps for Divine Protection

In times of spiritual need, calling upon Saint Michael's light can create a powerful aura of protection. The following is a step-by-step ritual that brings together elements from Psalm 91, Jewish protective traditions, and Saint Michael's radiant light. This practice serves as a proactive way to fortify oneself, harnessing the divine energy of Michael's guardianship.

Ritual of Protection Using Saint Michael's Light

Preparation and Sacred Setting

1. **Choose a Sacred Space**: Select a space where you feel secure, preferably in a quiet area where you won't be disturbed. Place objects that signify protection to you—this could be a Saint Michael statue, a blue candle, or a piece of clear quartz.
2. **Materials Needed**:
    - A blue or white candle (representing Michael's light and divine protection)
    - Psalm 91 text or a printed excerpt of its verses
    - Incense (frankincense or myrrh, traditionally associated with sanctification)
    - A small protective amulet or token, such as a piece of metal or a protective charm with Michael's name

3. **Centering and Intention Setting**: Begin by taking a few deep breaths to ground yourself. As you breathe, set a clear intention for protection and ask for Saint Michael's presence.

   Say aloud:

   > "Saint Michael, protector of divine justice, guardian of light, I invite your presence. Shield me from harm and surround me with your strength. May your light safeguard my path, repelling all that seeks to disturb my peace."

The Shielding Ritual

1. **Lighting the Candle and Incense**: Light the candle, allowing it to symbolize the beginning of Michael's protective light around you. Light the incense, wafting it gently in each direction to purify the space and set a sacred, peaceful atmosphere.
2. **Reciting Psalm 91**: Slowly read Psalm 91, visualizing Saint Michael's light forming a protective sphere around you. Focus especially on verse 11:

   > "He will command his angels concerning you to guard you in all your ways."

   Feel the words of the psalm resonating deeply, as if each verse strengthens the shield of protection around you.

3. **Calling Upon Saint Michael's Light**: Visualize a powerful, radiant blue-white light descending upon you, emanating from Saint Michael's sword and encircling you in a protective aura. Imagine this light forming a sphere, protecting you from any negative forces or harmful energies.

   Speak these words:

> "With Michael's light, I am shielded. No darkness shall touch me; no harm shall cross this boundary. His light, my fortress; his strength, my defense."

4. **Holding the Amulet or Token**: Take the protective amulet or token and hold it over the flame briefly, allowing it to absorb the light's energy. Visualize Saint Michael's energy sealing into the item, turning it into a constant, tangible symbol of his protective presence.

   Say:

   > "Saint Michael, may this token bear your strength, shielding me in every way. With it, I carry your protection close."

5. **Concluding and Setting Intention for Continued Protection**: Sit in the presence of the candlelight, visualizing your entire being encased in this sacred shield. When you are ready, say a closing prayer:

   > "Saint Michael, thank you for your protection, for the strength and peace you bring. May I walk forward with your shield around me, carrying your light always."

6. **Closure**: Extinguish the candle, envisioning the light sealing around you as an invisible shield that stays with you. Keep the amulet with you as a reminder of Michael's protection.

Integrating the Ritual's Power and Reflecting on Saint Michael's Presence

After the ritual, take a moment each day to reestablish this connection with Saint Michael's shield. Visualize his light encircling you during moments of vulnerability, reinforcing your resolve. Periodically touch the amulet or token to bring yourself back to the state of divine protection, grounding yourself in Michael's strength.

Daily Practice for Ongoing Protection:

1. **Morning Shielding Visualization:** As you start your day, take a moment to close your eyes and visualize Michael's light surrounding you. Repeat a simple affirmation, such as "I am protected by the light of Saint Michael," as you imagine a sphere of protection forming around you.
2. **Reflective Journaling:** Reflect in a journal about times you felt protected or moments when Michael's presence seemed particularly close. Journaling this process helps to build a stronger connection to his guidance.
3. **Renewing the Amulet's Power:** Every month or during challenging times, return to the ritual with the amulet. Re-bless it by holding it over a flame or reciting Psalm 91 again, reaffirming its protective energy.

Embracing Saint Michael's Protection in Everyday Life

The gift of Saint Michael's protection is not only a source of spiritual security but also an invitation to walk with greater courage and resilience. By invoking his light, we align ourselves with divine justice and the fortitude needed to face life's unseen forces. This ritual not only calls upon his guardianship but also teaches us the sacred strength within our own being, urging us to move forward in life with the assurance that we are shielded, supported, and guided by a power greater than any adversity we may face.

Purifying Flames: Saint Michael's Transformative Magic for Spiritual Cleansing and Renewal

Transformative magic, especially when guided by Saint Michael, is deeply rooted in the principles of purification and inner renewal. This form of magic addresses the need to clear spiritual blockages, release negativity, and activate one's highest potential. The path of purification, as taught by Saint Michael, uses fire and light as sacred symbols of transformation, offering an avenue to dissolve unwanted energies and rise into a state of spiritual clarity and strength.

The Symbolism of Purification Through Fire: Lessons from Isaiah 6:6-7

The imagery of purification through fire is vividly captured in the book of Isaiah, where the prophet encounters a seraph who touches his lips with a burning coal, symbolizing the cleansing of sin and impurity:

"Then one of the seraphim flew to me with a live coal in his hand, which he had taken with tongs from the altar. With it, he touched my mouth and said, 'See, this has touched your lips; your guilt is taken away and your sin atoned for.'" — *Isaiah 6:6-7*

In this passage, fire is not a destructive force but a transformative one, purifying Isaiah's soul and allowing him to stand with renewed clarity in the presence of the divine. This cleansing by fire reflects the nature of Saint Michael's transformative magic, which clears away spiritual impurities and facilitates deeper alignment with divine purpose.

Isaiah's experience reminds us that fire can act as a spiritual agent of change, burning away what is no longer needed, freeing us from guilt, and opening the way for growth and enlightenment. Invoking this symbolism, Saint Michael's transformative rituals invite us to release what holds us back and embrace a heightened sense of purity and purpose.

Kabbalistic Perspectives on Spiritual Purification

Kabbalistic teachings emphasize spiritual purification as an essential process for aligning with the Divine. The Zohar, a foundational Kabbalistic text, describes the need to cleanse the soul of accumulated impurities, comparing it to refining metals. In Kabbalah, purification prepares the individual for divine insight, enabling a clearer understanding of their soul's purpose and bringing them closer to God's light. The cleansing process is seen as necessary for transforming lower, material desires into spiritual awareness.

Saint Michael, as an archangel associated with divine justice, strength, and purification, guides us through these transformative processes. His connection to fire in Kabbalistic and mystical lore underscores his role as a guardian of spiritual renewal. In a ritualized practice of purification, Michael's influence can help practitioners cleanse their energy, purify their intentions, and enter a state of heightened spiritual awareness.

Invoking Saint Michael's Transformative Energy: Ritual of Purification Through Fire

To harness Saint Michael's transformative and purifying energy, the following ritual has been crafted to facilitate a deep spiritual cleanse, ridding oneself of negativity and invoking renewal. This ritual is ideal during times of transition, personal growth, or when one feels weighed down by spiritual blockages.

Preparation for the Ritual

1. **Create a Sacred Space**: Choose a quiet, undisturbed area where you feel at peace. Ideally, perform the ritual

near an open window or outdoors to allow for natural airflow. Arrange items associated with Saint Michael, such as a blue or red candle, a small bowl of salt, and a piece of incense, like frankincense, known for its purifying properties.
2. **Materials Needed**:
   - Blue or red candle (representing Michael's fire of transformation)
   - Small bowl of salt (symbolizing purification and grounding)
   - Frankincense incense (to invite a cleansing atmosphere)
   - A small piece of paper and a pen (for releasing specific intentions or energies)
   - A metal bowl or fireproof dish (for burning the paper safely)
3. **Set Intentions**: Before beginning, take a few moments to center yourself. Reflect on any negative energy, habits, or emotions you wish to release. Think about what you would like to purify and transform within yourself.

Say aloud:

> "Saint Michael, guardian of divine purity, I invite you to guide me through the sacred fires of transformation. Help me release what no longer serves, clearing my path to walk in harmony with my highest self."

Step-by-Step Ritual Instructions

1. Lighting the Candle and Incense: Initiating Transformation

Begin by lighting the candle and incense. Focus on the flame as a symbol of divine purity and transformation, inviting Saint Michael's presence into the space. Imagine the candle's flame as a direct connection to his light, providing the power needed to cleanse and renew.

Invocation:

"Saint Michael, protector and purifier, I call upon your transformative light. May this flame burn away negativity, clearing all that hinders me from divine clarity."

Allow the candle's light to fill you with a sense of courage, trust, and openness to change.

2. Holding the Salt: Grounding in Purification

Take a small pinch of salt, holding it between your fingers. Close your eyes and visualize the salt absorbing any lingering negative energies within you, grounding them as a force of earth and purity.

Say aloud:

"By the purity of earth, I release all negative energy, binding it to this salt to be grounded and neutralized."

Sprinkle the salt around the base of the candle, symbolizing a circle of purity that reinforces the sacred space.

3. Writing Intentions for Release: Clarifying Your Transformation

On the small piece of paper, write down anything specific you wish to release—whether it's fear, self-doubt, resentment, or past trauma. Be honest and clear, as this step marks the moment of acknowledgment and readiness to let go.

Say:

"With clarity, I acknowledge what I wish to release. May this intention be transformed by the light of Saint Michael, purified in divine fire."

As you hold the paper, visualize Michael's energy surrounding you, preparing to burn away these limitations.

4. Burning the Paper: Releasing into the Flame of Saint Michael

Hold the paper with your written intentions over the flame, allowing it to catch fire. Place it in the metal bowl to burn safely, watching the flames consume the paper. As it burns, imagine these limitations dissolving into the smoke, carried away by Michael's transformative energy.

Speak these words:

"Saint Michael, with your fire, I release these burdens. Let all that does not serve me be purified and transformed. May your light renew and guide me."

Allow yourself to feel a sense of liberation as the smoke rises, carrying away what you have released.

5. Reflective Meditation: Receiving the Cleansing Energy

After the paper has burned, sit quietly in the candle's light. Close your eyes and focus on your breathing, imagining each breath cleansing you further. Picture Michael's light enveloping your being, filling every cell with a renewed sense of peace, clarity, and spiritual alignment.

Silently affirm:

"I am renewed by the light of Saint Michael. His strength is within me; his purity is my guide."

Remain in this state for as long as you feel needed, absorbing the calm and clarity.

6. Closing the Ritual

When you feel ready, offer thanks to Saint Michael for his guidance and protection throughout this ritual. Extinguish the candle, visualizing the protective light sealing within you, ensuring ongoing clarity and resilience.

Closing words:

"Thank you, Saint Michael, for guiding me through transformation. May your light continue to purify and protect, guiding me toward divine truth."

Dispose of the ashes from the burned paper in the earth, symbolizing the final grounding and release of negativity.

Integrating Saint Michael's Transformative Energy

After the ritual, continue to invite Saint Michael's light into your life, especially when feelings of negativity or obstacles arise. Practicing ongoing spiritual cleansing will reinforce your sense of inner clarity and strength.

Daily Practice for Continued Purification

1. **Morning Invocation**: Begin each morning by visualizing Saint Michael's flame igniting within your heart, purifying your intentions and clearing your energy. Say a short affirmation, such as "I am guided by the light of Saint Michael, purified and protected."
2. **Weekly Salt Ritual**: Sprinkle a small amount of salt around your home or workspace weekly, reinforcing the space with Michael's protective presence. Imagine any stagnant or negative energy dissolving as it touches the salt.
3. **Reflection and Journaling**: Reflect regularly on any transformative moments or insights gained through this practice. Journaling your experiences will help you integrate the wisdom of Saint Michael's transformative

light, making the purification process a continuous journey of spiritual growth.

Embracing the Path of Transformation with Saint Michael

Saint Michael's teachings on transformation and purification remind us of the sacred power of release, inviting us to rise stronger and more aligned with our divine purpose. Each step on this path reinforces the courage needed to let go of what hinders us, creating a life centered in truth, strength, and clarity. By embracing Saint Michael's light, we commit ourselves to a lifelong journey of spiritual refinement, knowing that each moment of release is a sacred step toward realizing our highest potential.

Unveiling the Path of Truth: Saint Michael's Magic of Discernment and Liberation

In the quest for truth, Saint Michael stands as a beacon, guiding seekers through the shadows of uncertainty and deception. With a steadfast commitment to uncovering divine truth and illuminating the path to spiritual freedom, Michael's teachings on discernment offer profound insights into understanding the nature of reality and the hidden truths that lie beneath appearances. This form of magic encompasses the wisdom of ancient scriptures and mystical traditions, serving as a compass to those who seek clarity and liberation from illusions.

"The Truth Will Set You Free": A Scriptural Foundation for Discernment

In John 8:32, we find a foundational declaration of spiritual freedom through truth:

"You will know the truth, and the truth will set you free." — *John 8:32*

This verse reminds us that truth has the power to break chains of ignorance and deception, allowing us to align ourselves with divine clarity and authenticity. In the teachings of Saint Michael, truth-seeking is a sacred endeavor that requires courage and commitment, as it often involves confronting aspects of ourselves or the world that we may find uncomfortable. Michael, with his light and discernment, helps seekers navigate these complexities, providing the tools to discern truth from illusion.

For Michael, the pursuit of truth is not just a mental exercise but a deeply transformative experience that liberates the soul from inner and outer bonds. By connecting with his energy, we can gain insight, uncover hidden motivations, and achieve spiritual clarity that empowers us to make wise choices aligned with divine will.

Jewish and Kabbalistic Traditions on Discerning Truth

In Jewish and Kabbalistic traditions, the pursuit of truth is an essential aspect of spiritual development. The Hebrew word for truth, *emet*, is composed of the first, middle, and last letters of the Hebrew alphabet, symbolizing the completeness and unity of truth. According to Kabbalistic teachings, truth is seen as a divine principle that connects all realms, from the earthly to the celestial. Discerning truth requires a harmonious alignment of mind, heart, and soul, enabling one to see beyond illusions and perceive the divine essence in all things.

The Zohar, a central Kabbalistic text, describes the process of refining one's inner senses to perceive truth, suggesting that those who seek truth must purify their intentions and cultivate a heart of humility and openness. Saint Michael's teachings resonate with these principles, as he emphasizes the importance of inner purity and sincerity in the search for truth. By invoking his guidance, practitioners can gain insights that are not readily accessible through ordinary perception, uncovering deeper layers of reality and achieving spiritual clarity.

Invoking the Magic of Truth: A Ritual for Saint Michael's Guidance in Truth-Seeking

The following ritual is designed to invite Saint Michael's energy into the process of discernment, offering protection, insight, and clarity as you seek the truth within and around you. Through this practice, you will gain a heightened sense of awareness and an ability to perceive underlying truths that may be obscured by surface appearances.

Preparation for the Ritual

1. **Setting Your Intention**: Begin by clarifying your purpose for seeking truth. Reflect on what you hope to discover, whether it is clarity in a personal situation, insight into your spiritual path, or a deeper understanding of yourself. Keep your intention sincere and specific, as this will guide the energy of the ritual.
2. **Materials Needed**:
    - A white candle (representing purity and clarity)
    - A small mirror (symbolizing reflection and the ability to see clearly)
    - Frankincense or myrrh incense (to purify the space and enhance mental clarity)
    - A notebook and pen (for recording insights and reflections)
    - Optional: A small, clear quartz crystal (to amplify clarity and intention)
3. **Creating a Sacred Space**: Find a quiet, comfortable space where you can perform this ritual without interruptions. Place the candle and mirror before you,

along with the incense and any other items you may wish to use.

Invocation:

> "Saint Michael, guardian of divine truth, I invite your presence here. Help me to see with clarity and discernment, to uncover the truth that will set me free. Guide me with your light, so that I may walk the path of truth with courage and wisdom."

Step-by-Step Ritual Instructions

1. Lighting the Candle and Incense: Initiating Clarity

Light the white candle and the incense, allowing their light and scent to fill the space. Imagine this flame as a symbol of Saint Michael's clarity, illuminating the truth and clearing away any shadows of confusion or deception.

Say aloud:

"By the light of Saint Michael, I invoke clarity and insight. Let all shadows dissipate, and may only truth remain in my sight."

As the flame burns, focus on the intention to see beyond illusions and into the essence of whatever you seek to understand.

2. Gazing into the Mirror: Reflecting on Inner and Outer Truths

Take the mirror in your hands or place it where you can gaze into it comfortably. As you look at your reflection, allow yourself to soften your focus, not looking at your physical features but rather seeing into the deeper layers of yourself.

Contemplative Words:

"Mirror of truth, reveal to me the essence within and beyond. May I see not only the surface but the soul of all that I seek."

In this reflective state, allow any images, impressions, or thoughts to arise. Pay attention to the feelings that accompany these insights, as they may reveal underlying truths you have yet to recognize. Take several moments to meditate on what emerges, knowing that Michael's energy is guiding you.

3. Holding the Quartz Crystal (Optional): Amplifying Clarity

If you are using a clear quartz crystal, hold it in your hands and imagine it absorbing and amplifying the energy of clarity and truth. Picture Saint Michael's light filling the crystal, making it a beacon of pure insight.

Affirmation:

"Saint Michael, empower this crystal with the light of truth. May it hold and amplify clarity, guiding my mind and heart to discern with wisdom."

Hold the crystal near your heart or forehead, letting its energy assist you in connecting with your deeper intuition.

4. Writing Reflections: Documenting Insights and Truths

Take your notebook and write down any insights or revelations you received during the mirror meditation. This step is essential, as it allows you to capture fleeting thoughts that may hold significant meaning upon later reflection.

Suggested Writing Prompt:

"What truths did I uncover today? How do these truths guide me in understanding myself, others, or my path?"

Write freely, without censoring, as this process often brings subconscious insights to the surface. Revisit these notes later to deepen your understanding.

5. Closing Words and Gratitude to Saint Michael

When you feel ready, close the ritual by thanking Saint Michael for his guidance. Extinguish the candle, visualizing its light sealing within you the clarity and truth you have gained.

Closing Words:

"Thank you, Saint Michael, for your guidance and illumination. May your light of truth remain within me, guiding my path and strengthening my spirit."

Sit quietly for a few moments, allowing the insights and energy of the ritual to integrate within you.

Integrating Truth and Discernment in Daily Life

After the ritual, continue to work with the energy of discernment in your daily life. The following practices can help reinforce and deepen your connection to truth-seeking and inner clarity:

Daily Practice of Reflection and Self-Questioning

Each day, set aside a few minutes to reflect on moments where you were called to discern truth. Whether in conversations, decisions, or moments of inner doubt, ask yourself: "Am I seeing clearly, or am I being influenced by fear or attachment?" This practice will strengthen your ability to see beyond surface impressions.

Weekly Journaling for Discernment

Dedicate time each week to journal on any significant moments of clarity or insight. Reflect on how Saint Michael's guidance has helped you uncover truths, either about yourself or others. Use this time to document any patterns or recurring themes that arise in your pursuit of truth.

Honoring the Practice of Inner Silence

Spend a few moments each week in complete silence, allowing your mind to quiet and your awareness to sharpen. Saint Michael teaches that truth often reveals itself in the stillness, beyond the noise of daily life. By honoring moments of inner silence, you create a sacred space where truths can naturally arise.

Living in Alignment with Truth and Discernment

Living in alignment with truth as guided by Saint Michael is a path of courage and inner freedom. Each moment of clarity and discernment becomes a stepping stone toward a more authentic and spiritually empowered life. By committing to this journey, you embody Michael's light, becoming a vessel of truth that shines brightly in the world. This practice not only benefits your spiritual growth but also enhances your ability to serve others with integrity, compassion, and wisdom, reflecting the divine truth that Saint Michael holds as a guardian and guide.

Banishing and Balancing: The Art of Spiritual Cleansing and Integration with Saint Michael's Guidance

In the intricate dance of light and shadow, the power to balance and banish negativity is one of the most potent and essential forms of spiritual practice. From Saint Michael's perspective, the act of banishing is not merely about casting away darkness or unclean spirits, but about creating a sacred balance—a harmony that welcomes light while integrating and transforming shadow. Michael's teachings emphasize that true spiritual empowerment lies in understanding and mastering this balance, allowing us to live in harmony with ourselves and our surroundings. This knowledge draws on biblical wisdom, Jewish mystical practices, and Michael's own role as an archangelic force for justice and purification.

Casting Out Unclean Spirits: Lessons from Matthew 12:43-45

In the Gospel of Matthew, Jesus speaks of the nature of unclean spirits and the importance of filling spaces with positive energy and purpose:

"When an unclean spirit goes out of a person, it passes through waterless places seeking rest, but finds none. Then it says, 'I will return to my house from which I came.' And when it comes, it finds it empty, swept, and put in order. Then it goes and brings with it seven other spirits more evil than itself, and they enter and dwell there; and the last state of that person is worse than the first." — *Matthew 12:43-45*

This passage illustrates a profound truth about banishment and spiritual balance: clearing out negative energies or entities alone is not enough. Spaces—both physical and spiritual—must be filled with intentional, positive forces to prevent negativity from returning. Saint Michael teaches that banishment should be followed by consecration and alignment with divine energy, ensuring that the cleansed space becomes a sanctuary of light and purpose. By seeking Michael's guidance, practitioners can gain the wisdom needed to both dispel negativity and bring harmony into their lives.

Jewish Mystical Practices for Spiritual Cleansing and Balance

In Jewish mysticism, the act of banishing or purifying a space is deeply woven into the practice of maintaining spiritual cleanliness. Rituals such as reciting blessings, burning incense, and using water or salt as purifying agents are common practices in Jewish traditions to ward off harmful energies. These rituals also reflect the intention of reestablishing divine order, as cleanliness in the physical realm is seen as reflective of purity in the spiritual realm.

Saint Michael's teachings resonate with these practices, as he instructs on the importance of intentionality and reverence in spiritual cleansing. By treating each space as sacred and each ritual act as a connection to divine energy, practitioners can create environments that reflect and amplify their highest intentions.

Balancing and Banishment Ritual: A Step-by-Step Guide

This ritual combines elements of banishment and blessing, using Michael's guidance to cast out negativity and bring balance. Through this practice, you'll create a protective shield of light, removing lingering shadows and integrating the transformative energy of Saint Michael.

Preparation for the Ritual

1. **Setting Your Intention**: Before beginning, take a few moments to clarify your purpose. Reflect on what you hope to clear or release, and visualize the space as a sanctuary of peace and harmony. Set an intention to not only remove negativity but to welcome divine balance and healing.
2. **Gathering Materials**:
    - White candle (for purity and Michael's light)

- Small bowl of salt or consecrated water (for cleansing)
- Incense (such as frankincense or myrrh for purification)
- Bell or small drum (to raise energy and clear stagnant energies)
- Mirror or clear quartz crystal (to reflect and amplify Michael's energy)
- Optional: Protective symbol (such as a cross, Star of David, or Michael's sigil)

3. **Creating a Sacred Space**: Begin in a quiet, undisturbed place. Arrange the materials in a circle or in a position that feels centered. Light the candle and incense, inviting Michael's presence to guide and protect the ritual.

Step-by-Step Ritual Instructions

1. Invoking Saint Michael and Setting Protection

Begin by lighting the candle and calling upon Saint Michael to guide the ritual. As you light the candle, visualize his protective light encircling the space, dispelling any shadows.

Say aloud:

"Saint Michael, guardian of light and justice, I call upon you now. Surround this space with your presence, casting out all shadows and filling it with divine peace. Guide me in this act of banishment and balance, that I may create a sanctuary of harmony and strength."

Feel the energy in the room begin to shift, as if Michael's light has entered, creating a boundary against negativity.

2. Using Salt or Water for Cleansing

Take the bowl of salt or consecrated water. If using salt, sprinkle it lightly around the perimeter of the room or area you are cleansing. If using water, dip your fingers in the water and gently flick it around the room. This action purifies and seals the space.

Say:

"With this element, I cleanse and protect. May all impurities be washed away, leaving only light and peace."

Visualize the salt or water absorbing any negative energy, dissolving it completely, and fortifying the room with protective energy.

3. Sound Cleansing with the Bell or Drum

Take the bell or drum and begin to gently sound it, starting at one side of the room and moving clockwise. Sound vibrations are powerful for dispelling stagnant energy, as they shake loose any lingering negativity.

Recite:

"With sound, I awaken light and clear away all that does not serve. In Saint Michael's name, I call forth balance and peace."

Allow the sound to reverberate through the space, filling it with clarity and shaking loose any energies that are not aligned with your intention.

4. Gazing into the Mirror or Crystal: Reflecting Michael's Light

Hold the mirror or clear quartz crystal at the center of the room, allowing it to capture the light of the candle. Picture Michael's light shining through the mirror or crystal, amplifying clarity and protection.

Contemplative Words:

"May Saint Michael's light reflect throughout this space, illuminating truth and dispelling shadow. Let this room be a sanctuary of balance, where only love and wisdom dwell."

Hold this vision for several breaths, imagining the room filled with Michael's pure, protective light.

5. Closing with a Blessing and Symbol of Protection

As a final act, hold your chosen protective symbol (cross, Star of David, or Michael's sigil) over your heart and speak a blessing over the space.

Closing Words:

"By the guidance of Saint Michael, this space is now sealed in divine balance. May all who enter here be blessed, and may the light of truth protect and uplift this sanctuary."

Place the symbol somewhere in the room as a reminder of the ritual's intention, anchoring the balance and protection into the space.

Reflecting and Integrating the Ritual's Power

Once the ritual is complete, sit quietly, allowing yourself to feel the shift in energy within the space. Notice any sense of peace, clarity, or release that comes over you.

Daily Integration Practices

1. **Morning Grounding and Protection Visualization**

   Begin each day with a simple visualization: imagine yourself encircled by the light of Saint Michael, shielding you from any negativity while inviting positive energy to flow through you. This practice aligns you with the protective energy you created in the ritual, serving as a daily shield.

2. **Weekly Space Renewal and Blessing**

   To maintain the balance created in the ritual, take a few moments each week to refresh the space. Light the same candle and recite a brief blessing, reminding yourself and the space of your intention for peace and harmony.

Journaling Insights and Reflections

Reflect on any changes you notice within yourself or the space. Journaling provides a valuable opportunity to document subtle shifts and gain insights into your journey with Saint Michael's teachings on balance and banishment.

Embracing Michael's Teachings of Balance and Banishment in Everyday Life

The art of balancing and banishing negativity, as taught by Saint Michael, extends beyond ritual practice and into everyday life. With his guidance, you become empowered to confront and integrate your own shadows, transforming them into sources of strength and wisdom. This path of spiritual empowerment reminds us that every act of banishment is an opportunity to renew our commitment to balance and to cultivate harmony within ourselves and our surroundings. As you continue to work with Michael, may you carry his light, becoming a living vessel of divine balance and strength in the world.

Elemental and Archangelic Magic: Harnessing the Powers of Nature Through Saint Michael

The art of elemental and archangelic magic connects practitioners to the fundamental forces of nature, guided by the unique energies embodied by the archangels. Saint Michael, as the Archangel of Fire, represents the transformative power of courage, resilience, and divine strength. This understanding of elemental alignment not only empowers personal growth but also attunes the practitioner to the sacred dance between natural forces and divine intention.

Psalm 104:4 offers a poetic introduction to the elemental connection of angels: *"He makes his angels winds, his ministers a flaming fire."* Here, the association between angels and elemental forces highlights a profound truth within the cosmic order. Just as angels are expressions of divine will, elements are manifestations of creation's energy. Working with Michael's elemental aspect of fire allows us to tap into this dynamic energy, transforming inner darkness, sparking courage, and realigning ourselves with divine purpose.

Michael's Elemental Domain: Fire as a Force of Courage and Transformation

Fire, as an element, has long been revered as both a physical and spiritual force of transformation. Michael, with his sword of flame, embodies this fiery energy in its purest form. Fire's nature is to burn away impurities, reveal hidden truths, and instill a sense of resilience in those who work with it. In Michael's teachings, fire becomes a symbolic and literal means of overcoming fear, igniting passion, and seeking clarity amidst uncertainty.

Through the fire element, Michael's guidance channels a powerful current that transcends physical limitations, igniting inner courage and resilience. His connection to fire is also a reminder that, just as fire can destroy, it can also create anew, clearing the way for growth and revelation.

Archangels and the Elements: Insights from Jewish Lore on Angelic Forces and Directions

In Jewish mystical tradition, each of the four elements—earth, water, air, and fire—corresponds with specific archangels who govern these natural forces. This connection roots archangels not only in the heavens but within the physical world, as divine guardians of creation's energy. Traditionally, each direction (north, south, east, and west) aligns with an element, creating a sacred balance around the practitioner.

Michael's elemental association with fire situates him in the south, a position of active strength and transformation. This southern alignment emphasizes fire's power to overcome obstacles, just as Michael's own protective nature seeks to shield against darkness and negative forces. Through ritual practice, the practitioner can draw upon this southern energy to instill courage and overcome personal fears, uniting Michael's guidance with the elemental force of fire.

The Ritual of Fire: Awakening Michael's Flame Within

This ritual invokes Saint Michael's fire element for personal transformation and courage. Through it, practitioners seek to release fear, spark inner resilience, and align their intentions with divine purpose. As a spiritual exercise, this ritual also serves to deepen one's connection to the elements and the archangels, creating a sacred alignment with Michael's protective fire.

Preparing for the Ritual

1. **Setting Your Intention**: Spend a few moments in quiet reflection, focusing on what you wish to transform or overcome. Visualize the outcome you seek, as if it has already come to pass. Set a clear intention to connect with Michael's fire to cleanse and empower your spirit.
2. **Gathering Materials**:
    - A red or white candle (symbolizing Michael's flame and purity)

- A small piece of charcoal or ash (for representing transformation and letting go of past limitations)
- Frankincense or sandalwood incense (for invoking sacred fire energy)
- A symbol of Michael (such as a small sword, shield, or Michael's sigil)
- A fire-safe bowl or container

3. **Creating a Sacred Circle**: Begin by lighting the candle in the southern part of your sacred space. This aligns with the elemental direction of fire and Michael's southern guardianship. Position your materials nearby in a way that feels respectful and intentional.

Step-by-Step Ritual Instructions

1. Invocation of Michael's Presence

Start by lighting the incense, allowing its scent to permeate the space, creating a sacred environment for the ritual. As you light the candle, visualize Michael's protective flame surrounding you, dispelling fear and negativity.

Invocation:

"Saint Michael, guardian of fire and courage, I call upon your light to surround and protect me. Ignite within me the strength to overcome all fear, to rise above all doubt. May your flame cleanse and transform, leading me to greater clarity and purpose."

Take a deep breath, feeling the energy in the room grow warmer and brighter as Michael's presence fills the space.

2. Symbolic Cleansing with Ash or Charcoal

Hold the piece of charcoal or ash in your hands, envisioning it absorbing all negative thoughts, fears, or limitations you wish to release. Visualize these obstacles flowing from your mind and heart into the charcoal.

Words of Release:

"With this symbol of ash, I release all that holds me back. Just as fire turns darkness to light, may Saint Michael's flame transform my fears into courage, my doubts into faith."

Place the ash or charcoal in the fire-safe bowl, symbolizing your willingness to surrender these limitations to the fire of Michael's guidance.

3. Lighting the Flame of Transformation

Holding your hands near the candle, close your eyes and imagine the flame's warmth spreading through your body, filling you with strength. Feel its energy reaching into every part of you, dissolving fears and filling you with unwavering courage.

Affirmation:

"As Michael's flame, I rise renewed. Fear holds no power over me; courage fills my heart, and strength guides my steps. In the fire of transformation, I become who I am meant to be."

Repeat this affirmation as many times as feels right, allowing its energy to resonate deeply within you.

4. Reflective Gazing into the Flame

Gaze softly into the candle flame, seeing it as a symbol of your own inner fire, an ever-present source of strength and resilience. In this moment of reflection, ask Michael to reveal any insights or guidance you need.

Prayer for Guidance:

"Saint Michael, let your light reveal my path. May I walk with courage, transformed by the fire of your wisdom and protection."

Spend a few moments in silence, observing any thoughts, images, or feelings that arise, trusting that they come from Michael's guidance.

5. Closing with Gratitude and Integration

When you feel ready, thank Michael for his presence and the gift of courage he has bestowed. Visualize the flame's energy settling into your heart, a permanent source of strength you can draw upon in times of need.

Words of Gratitude:

"Thank you, Saint Michael, for your strength and your light. May your fire guide me always, a source of courage and transformation in all I do."

Extinguish the candle, symbolizing the integration of this transformative energy within yourself. If desired, keep the symbol of Michael nearby as a reminder of this connection.

Integrating the Ritual's Energy into Daily Life

To carry forward the courage and resilience from this ritual, establish small daily practices that reinforce Michael's transformative fire within.

Morning Invocation of Michael's Fire

Each morning, visualize Michael's flame within your heart, illuminating your path for the day. Repeat a simple affirmation, such as *"With Michael's fire, I walk in courage and strength,"* to align yourself with his energy.

Weekly Fire Cleansing

On a weekly basis, relight the candle from the ritual and spend a few moments reconnecting with the energy of courage and resilience. Use this time to release any new doubts or fears that may have arisen, keeping Michael's fire active in your life.

Reflective Journaling on Transformation

In a journal, document moments when you felt empowered by courage or clarity. Reflect on how Michael's teachings and this ritual's energy have influenced your actions and mindset, solidifying the changes you have initiated.

Embracing Michael's Fire Element for Lifelong Transformation

By working with Michael's fire, practitioners gain a deeper understanding of courage, resilience, and the sacred cycle of transformation. This connection with the fire element helps dissolve personal fears and instills an enduring strength, guiding you through challenges and preparing you for growth. Saint Michael's flame is more than a ritual tool; it is a lifelong source of divine guidance, igniting purpose, and revealing your highest potential. As you continue on this path, may Michael's fire light your way, empowering you to walk through life with the courage and conviction of divine protection and purpose.

Consecration and Protection of Magical Tools: Aligning with Divine Purpose Through Saint Michael

In spiritual practice, magical tools hold significant power and are conduits of intention and divine energy. However, before they can be used effectively, these tools must be properly consecrated and protected, aligning them with higher purposes and keeping them free from disruptive energies. Consecrating tools not only prepares them for sacred work but also allows practitioners to connect deeply with their tools, fostering an intentional and spiritually fortified practice.

This approach to consecration and protection is inspired by Saint Michael's teachings, emphasizing purity, alignment, and divine protection. The process draws on both biblical references, such as Exodus 30:25-29, where God instructed Moses on consecrating sacred objects, and Jewish ritual practices, which offer structured ways to bless and guard spiritual items. Michael, as a guardian and purifier, lends his energy and authority to these practices, ensuring that each consecrated tool serves its intended purpose with integrity.

Consecration as Spiritual Alignment: Insights from Exodus 30

The process of consecrating sacred items has a strong precedent in Exodus 30:25-29, where God gives Moses specific instructions for anointing sacred objects. In this passage, Moses is commanded to blend spices and olive oil to create a holy anointing oil, which is then applied to the tabernacle, altar, and other sacred objects to make them holy. This act of anointing serves not only as a way to purify the objects but also as a means to dedicate them solely to divine use, setting them apart from all other items.

In the context of consecrating magical tools, the same principle applies: the act of consecration transforms ordinary objects into sacred ones, making them suitable for spiritual practice. This ritual draws upon the purity of Saint Michael's guidance to help practitioners dedicate their tools, sealing them with divine purpose and protection.

Jewish Ritual Practices of Blessing and Protection: The Role of Intention and Sacred Words

Jewish ritual practices for blessing and protection of items involve focused intention and specific blessings. Items are traditionally blessed through prayer, anointing, or laying on of hands, imbuing them with sanctity and divine purpose. This tradition, deeply rooted in Kabbalistic teachings, holds that spoken blessings anchor divine energy into physical objects, preserving them against negativity and enhancing their sacred purpose.

In following this approach, practitioners may use prayers that reflect Saint Michael's role as protector and purifier. Through spoken blessings and sacred gestures, tools become linked to Michael's strength, aligning them with higher intentions.

Michael's Role in Consecrating Tools for Spiritual Alignment

Saint Michael's guardianship extends to every aspect of spiritual practice, including the tools used within it. Michael's energy serves as a shield against unclean or harmful forces, ensuring that consecrated objects remain focused on the divine intentions for which they were dedicated. Invoking his presence in this ritual affirms the practitioner's commitment to using these tools responsibly and with reverence. Michael's influence sanctifies and protects these items, imbuing them with purity, strength, and spiritual clarity.

Ritual of Consecration and Protection: Establishing Divine Alignment

This consecration ritual is designed to prepare your spiritual tools, allowing them to be used for sacred work with the blessing and protection of Saint Michael. The ritual incorporates elements of anointing, prayer, and invocation, each serving to anchor divine energy within your tools.

Preparation for the Ritual

1. **Define the Purpose of Your Tools**: Begin by setting clear intentions for each tool you are consecrating. Consider how you will use them—whether for divination, protection, transformation, or another purpose. Write down these intentions, as this will help clarify the energy you wish to infuse into each item.
2. **Gathering Materials**:
    - Olive oil or another sacred anointing oil (symbolizing purity and dedication)
    - Frankincense or myrrh incense (for purification)
    - A small white cloth or silk (to wrap and protect the tools after consecration)
    - A candle dedicated to Michael, ideally blue or white
    - An image or symbol of Saint Michael (such as a small statue or icon) to represent his presence during the ritual
    - Your magical tools placed nearby in your sacred space
3. **Create a Sacred Space**: Set up your space with the candle and symbol of Saint Michael. Place the incense so that its smoke will envelop your tools, symbolizing the presence of divine protection.

Step-by-Step Ritual Instructions

1. Invocation of Saint Michael and Sacred Intention

Begin by lighting the candle and incense, creating a sacred atmosphere. Face the tools before you and center yourself, breathing deeply to attune to the present moment.

Invocation:

"Saint Michael, Archangel of protection and purity, I call upon your presence to guard and consecrate these sacred tools. May they serve their purpose with divine alignment, free from all impurity and negativity. Guide my hands and intentions, that I may consecrate each item in your light and strength."

Pause to feel Michael's protective energy surrounding you, as if a shield of light encompasses the space.

2. Purification with Incense

Pass each tool through the incense smoke, visualizing any negative or unwanted energies dissolving. Imagine the smoke creating a layer of purity around each item.

Words of Purification:

"With this sacred smoke, I cleanse these tools of all impurities. By Michael's grace, they are free from all influences, ready to serve in alignment with divine purpose."

Allow the incense to continue burning as you move into the next steps.

3. Anointing and Consecrating the Tools with Oil

Take a small amount of anointing oil on your fingertip. Gently touch each tool, making the sign of a cross, star, or other symbol meaningful to you. As you anoint each tool, visualize it becoming filled with light and purpose, dedicated to serving your spiritual path under Saint Michael's guidance.

Words of Consecration:

"By this sacred oil, I consecrate [name of tool] in Saint Michael's name. May it be a vessel of divine purpose, aligned with purity, protection, and truth. Let it serve with integrity, a reflection of Michael's light."

Repeat for each tool, speaking its purpose aloud and feeling the energy of dedication with each anointing.

4. Blessing with Saint Michael's Light

Holding your hands over the tools, imagine a beam of radiant blue light flowing down from above, enveloping each item in Saint Michael's energy. Feel this light sealing the tools, rendering them invulnerable to negative forces and aligned with divine will.

Blessing Prayer:

"Saint Michael, may your light shield and bless these tools, infusing them with your strength and purpose. May they remain pure and steadfast, serving only the highest intentions. Let your protection guard them always, that they may be used in harmony with divine truth."

Allow the light to settle, feeling each tool radiate with a sense of completeness and readiness for sacred work.

5. Wrapping and Storing the Tools

Gently wrap each consecrated tool in the white cloth or silk, symbolizing the preservation of their purity. This covering acts as a physical reminder of the protection and blessing imbued into each item.

Words of Closure:

"With gratitude, I thank you, Saint Michael, for your guidance and protection. May these tools remain in your care, aligned and guarded by your strength. Let them serve with integrity, as instruments of divine light."

Extinguish the candle, visualizing the energy from the ritual sealing into each item, ensuring that its consecration endures.

Post-Ritual Integration and Reflection

After the ritual, spend a few moments in silence, attuning to the energy shift around your newly consecrated tools. Reflect on your intentions for each item, and consider journaling any thoughts or impressions that arose during the ritual. Allow yourself to feel confident in the strength and alignment of these tools, knowing they have been fortified under Saint Michael's protection.

Daily Affirmation of Protection

To reinforce the consecration, begin each practice session by holding your tools and saying, *"With Michael's light, I honor the purpose of these tools. May they serve with purity and protection."* This small ritual reconnects you with the energy set during consecration.

Monthly Re-Consecration

Consider re-consecrating your tools monthly, especially if you use them frequently. This practice maintains their energetic integrity, keeping them attuned to your spiritual intentions.

Living in Alignment with Michael's Consecration Energy

Consecration, as taught through Saint Michael, is more than a ritual—it is an ongoing commitment to align oneself with divine purpose. Through the regular use of consecrated tools, practitioners are reminded of the sacred partnership with Michael's energy, fostering a deep sense of alignment, purity, and strength. Each time you reach for these tools, remember the transformative power of consecration, seeing it as a channel that continuously connects your practice to the divine, with Michael as your protector and guide.

With every consecrated item, you hold a piece of this dedication, a reminder that spiritual tools are not just objects but vessels carrying divine intention, purified and guarded by the unwavering presence of Saint Michael. May each use of these tools inspire you to walk with confidence, purpose, and a deeper connection to the sacred.

Invoking the Power of Saint Michael: A Ritual for Guidance and Protection

Invoking Saint Michael's presence is a profound act of calling upon divine strength, clarity, and protection. Known as the defender of souls and the guardian of divine order, Michael's role in spiritual tradition is central to upholding justice, safeguarding against malevolent forces, and empowering individuals to face their own battles with courage and resilience. This ritual, drawing from the biblical symbolism of Michael's battle in *Revelation 12:7*, alongside Jewish and Christian prayers, is designed to invoke his powerful guidance and protection.

This ritual serves as both a protective measure and a way to seek Michael's wisdom in times of uncertainty or spiritual conflict. Through careful preparation, heartfelt invocation, and deep reflection, practitioners align themselves with Saint Michael's strength, inviting his presence and fortifying their spiritual journey.

Michael's Divine Battle: *Revelation 12:7* as an Archetype of Spiritual Protection

The imagery of *Revelation 12:7* captures Michael as the celestial warrior, leading the forces of heaven against the dragon, a symbol of chaos and evil:

"Then war broke out in heaven. Michael and his angels fought against the dragon, and the dragon and his angels fought back."

This powerful verse symbolizes the eternal battle between light and darkness, order and chaos. In calling upon Michael through invocation, practitioners participate in this archetype, embracing the courage and resilience embodied by Michael. This ritual is a means to connect with the archangel's unwavering determination and commitment to divine order, an energy that can fortify practitioners in times of challenge and protect them from harm.

Sacred Tradition of Prayers to Saint Michael: Foundations in Jewish and Christian Devotion

Invocations to Saint Michael have ancient roots in both Jewish and Christian traditions. In Christian liturgy, prayers to Michael seek his protection and strength, especially in the face of temptation or spiritual adversity. Jewish mystical teachings acknowledge Michael as the "Prince of Mercy," a high-ranking angel who intercedes on behalf of humanity, offering divine protection and justice.

Prayers to Michael are therefore not merely protective chants but affirmations of divine justice, mercy, and the triumph of good over evil. By invoking these prayers, practitioners align themselves with an ancient lineage of faith and trust in Michael's guardianship.

Preparing for the Invocation Ritual: Gathering Materials and Setting Intentions

This ritual requires deliberate preparation to foster a receptive, sacred atmosphere. Each preparatory step serves to ground and focus the practitioner, setting the stage for a powerful invocation.

Materials for the Ritual

1. **A Blue or White Candle**: Symbolizing Michael's purity, protection, and strength.

2. **Frankincense or Myrrh Incense**: These scents purify the space and invite a sense of divine presence.
3. **Holy Water or Salt**: Used to cleanse the space and reinforce boundaries of protection.
4. **A Symbol of Saint Michael**: This could be an icon, a small statue, or even an image of Michael in battle.
5. **Bible or Prayer Book**: To read the scripture and prayers during the invocation.

Setting Sacred Space

1. **Create a Circle of Light**: Place the candle, incense, and symbol of Michael on a small altar or table, arranging them thoughtfully to form a circle of sacred light.
2. **Center Yourself**: Stand or sit comfortably, breathing deeply to calm the mind and center the heart. Visualize a blue light surrounding you, embodying Michael's protective energy.

Intention Setting: Before beginning, focus on your intention for the ritual. This might be a request for guidance, protection from negativity, or courage to face an upcoming challenge. Setting a clear intention aligns your energy with Michael's purpose and creates a channel for his presence to manifest.

The Invocation Ritual to Saint Michael: Step-by-Step Guide

This ritual is divided into three parts: Invocation, Reception of Michael's Presence, and Closure.

1. Invoking Saint Michael's Presence

Begin by lighting the candle and incense, symbolizing the beginning of a sacred interaction. Raise your hands or place them over your heart as a sign of openness to Michael's guidance.

Invocation of Michael:

"Saint Michael the Archangel, champion of light and defender of souls, I call upon your presence. As you battled the dragon in heaven, so too I seek your protection against the darkness that surrounds me. Stand beside me, guide me, shield me with your strength, that I may walk in courage and faith."

After this invocation, take a few breaths, feeling the energy in the room shift as you call upon Michael's presence.

2. Reading of Revelation 12:7 and Symbolic Reflection

Open your Bible to *Revelation 12:7* and read aloud:

"Then war broke out in heaven. Michael and his angels fought against the dragon, and the dragon and his angels fought back."

As you read, visualize Michael standing alongside you, his sword gleaming with light, ready to defend and protect. Feel his energy permeating the space, filling you with strength and determination.

3. Jewish and Christian Prayers of Protection

Recite a traditional prayer from Jewish or Christian sources, affirming Michael's role as protector and guardian.

Jewish Prayer of Protection (from *Siddur*, adapted):

"May the angel Michael be at my right, Gabriel at my left, Uriel before me, Raphael behind me, and above my head the Shekinah, the Divine Presence."

Or,

Christian Prayer to Saint Michael:

"Saint Michael the Archangel, defend us in battle. Be our protection against the wickedness and snares of the devil. May God rebuke him, we humbly pray, and do thou, O Prince of the heavenly hosts, by the power of God, cast into hell Satan and all the evil spirits who prowl about the world seeking the ruin of souls."

Let these words deepen your connection to Michael, affirming his guardianship over your life.

4. Envisioning Michael's Shield of Light

Close your eyes and imagine a shield of brilliant blue light forming around you, infused with Michael's protective energy. Visualize this light creating an impenetrable barrier, guarding you from all harm and negativity.

Words to Anchor the Shield:

"By Saint Michael's shield, I am protected. No harm shall enter, no darkness shall prevail. I stand within this circle of light, safe, guarded, and strong."

Spend several moments immersed in this light, allowing yourself to feel completely safe and secure.

Closure of the Invocation Ritual: Sealing the Protection and Gratitude

After you have completed the invocation and received Michael's presence, it is important to formally close the ritual, thanking him for his guidance and protection.

1. **Expressing Gratitude**: Bow your head or place your hands over your heart in a gesture of thanks.

    "Thank you, Saint Michael, for your presence, your strength, and your protection. May your guidance remain with me, guarding me as I walk my path."

2. **Sealing with Holy Water or Salt**: Sprinkle a bit of holy water or salt around the space, sealing the energy. This creates a tangible boundary, affirming the protection you have invoked.
3. **Extinguishing the Candle**: As you blow out the candle, visualize Michael's protective light remaining with you, even as the ritual concludes.

Words to Close:

"With Michael's blessing, I am safe. This ritual is complete, yet his protection endures."

Post-Ritual Reflection and Spiritual Fortification

After completing the ritual, spend some time in quiet reflection, allowing the energy of the invocation to settle. Journaling your experience can help you integrate any insights or messages that came through during the ritual. Reflect on how Michael's presence felt—whether it was a sense of warmth, strength, or clarity.

Daily Affirmation of Protection: To continue the effects of this ritual, use a brief daily affirmation:

"Saint Michael's shield surrounds me. I am safe, guided, and protected."

Repeating this affirmation reminds you of Michael's constant presence, helping you to embody the strength and courage that he inspires.

Weekly Renewal of Intentions: Once a week, light a candle and read *Revelation 12:7*, briefly re-invoking Michael's protection. This small act reinforces your connection to Michael and keeps his presence active in your life.

Living with Michael's Guidance: Embodying Courage and Faith

In calling upon Saint Michael, we do not only seek external protection but also open ourselves to embody his qualities of courage, resilience, and unwavering faith. By performing this invocation ritual, you align yourself with Michael's energy, becoming a vessel of strength and compassion. Let his presence guide you in moments of challenge, reminding you that you are never alone. As you walk forward, carry Michael's light within, knowing that his guidance and protection are only a prayer away.

As we move from practical applications of Saint Michael's guidance in spiritual and magickal practices, our focus now shifts to a rich exploration of the scriptural and mystical texts that give depth and historical context to his role. In this next section, *Scriptural Integration and Contextual References*, we delve into both canonical and non-canonical sources to uncover how Michael's purpose has been portrayed and honored across different religious traditions and texts. By examining Old Testament references, New Testament insights, Jewish mystical perspectives, and apocryphal accounts, we gain a multidimensional view of Michael's influence as protector, guide, and warrior. This exploration illuminates the ways in which Michael's role has been woven into the fabric of spiritual tradition, allowing us to integrate these powerful perspectives into a deeper, more historically anchored understanding of his presence.

7. Scriptural Foundations of Saint Michael's Role: Perspectives from Canonical and Mystical Texts

In this section, we turn to the foundational texts and scriptural references that illuminate Saint Michael's role as protector, guide, and advocate across spiritual traditions. By exploring key passages from the Old and New Testaments, the rich tapestry of Jewish mystical writings, and lesser-known apocryphal texts, we uncover how Michael's purpose has been recognized and revered over centuries. Each scriptural layer adds depth to our understanding of Michael, from his steadfast protection of Israel in the Book of Daniel to his powerful stance against evil in Revelation, and through the insights of mystical works like the Talmud and the Zohar. This exploration not only highlights Michael's enduring influence but also invites us to connect with his presence through the wisdom of ancient traditions, enabling a grounded, spiritually resonant approach to his teachings and guidance.

Old Testament Perspectives on Michael's Role: Protection, Guidance, and Divine Advocacy

The Old Testament, along with its extended apocryphal texts, offers a profound lens into Saint Michael's sacred role as protector and guide, revealing layers of his spiritual authority and purpose. Through scriptural references in books like Daniel and interpretive insights in texts such as the Book of Jubilees, Michael is presented not merely as an angelic figure but as a guardian of divine justice and a steadfast defender of humanity. Understanding Michael's role within these texts enables us to appreciate the depth of his spiritual mission and offers unique perspectives for practitioners seeking to connect with his energy.

Daniel 12:1 – Michael as the Protector of the People

The Book of Daniel is one of the most significant sources for understanding Saint Michael's protective role, particularly Daniel 12:1, which describes Michael as the "great prince" who stands guard over God's people during times of great distress:

"At that time Michael, the great prince who protects your people, will arise. There will be a time of distress such as has not happened from the beginning of nations until then. But at that time your people—everyone whose name is found written in the book—will be delivered." (Daniel 12:1, NIV)

Michael's Protective Role in Context

In this passage, Daniel's prophecy offers a glimpse into Michael's cosmic guardianship, portraying him as a powerful figure who rises to defend the people in their most desperate hour. The "time of distress" suggests a period of immense spiritual and earthly challenge, aligning with the apocalyptic vision Daniel presents. This scene is not only a forecast of divine intervention but an invitation to see Michael as a symbol of resilience, strength, and unwavering protection amid hardship.

Daniel's text reinforces the Jewish and later Christian view of Michael as a powerful spiritual warrior and advocate, bridging the divine and human realms. His role as protector of the faithful signifies an allegiance to divine justice, and by "arising" in times of trouble, Michael becomes a beacon of hope and courage for all who seek his guidance.

Ritual of Protection Inspired by Daniel 12:1

This ritual draws upon the themes of divine protection and deliverance found in Daniel 12:1, allowing practitioners to call upon Michael's guardianship in times of personal or collective crisis.

Purpose: To invoke Saint Michael's protective energy in times of spiritual distress or to seek courage when facing a personal challenge.

Materials Needed:

- A white candle (symbolizing Michael's divine light and protection)
- A small, unadorned stone or crystal to represent resilience
- Frankincense incense (to purify and call upon divine presence)
- A copy of Daniel 12:1 (or the text written on paper)

Preparation: Find a quiet space free of distractions, preferably near an open window or outside under the sky, to align with the concept of cosmic guardianship. Place the stone and candle in front of you, with the scripture passage nearby. Light the incense, allowing the smoke to represent the spiritual veil parting as you enter a sacred space.

Step-by-Step Instructions:

1. **Centering and Invocation**
   Begin by lighting the candle, focusing on its light as a representation of Michael's presence. Close your eyes and take several deep breaths, visualizing a radiant, protective light surrounding you.

   Say:
   "Saint Michael, protector of the faithful, I call upon your presence in this time of need. Arise as my

defender, as you did for the people in times past. Stand with me, shield me, and strengthen me with your divine light."

2. **Reciting Daniel 12:1**
   Slowly read Daniel 12:1, allowing each word to resonate deeply within you. Imagine Michael arising, his energy expanding and surrounding you as a protective shield. Feel his presence as a source of both defense and peace.
3. **Stone of Resilience**
   Hold the stone or crystal in your hands, visualizing it absorbing Michael's strength. Envision this object becoming a touchstone of courage and a reminder of divine protection.

   Say:
   "As this stone endures, so shall I endure. Michael, grant me your resilience to withstand all trials. Let this stone carry your strength and remind me of your guardianship."

4. **Prayer for Deliverance**
   With eyes closed, visualize any distress or challenges you face dissolving in Michael's light. Imagine his energy not only shielding you but uplifting you, carrying away fears or doubts.

   Say:
   "In your light, I am safe. In your strength, I am steadfast. Protect me, guide me, and deliver me through this time of trial. With gratitude, I accept your shield of courage and love."

5. **Closing**
   Allow the candle to burn down partially, symbolizing the continuation of Michael's protective energy in your life. Extinguish it when ready, placing the stone somewhere meaningful as a reminder of Michael's enduring presence.

Post-Ritual Reflection
After performing this ritual, reflect on Michael's protective qualities in your life. Carry the stone with you or place it somewhere visible to remind you of the strength and protection available to you. In moments of doubt, hold the stone, recall Daniel 12:1, and reaffirm your connection with Michael's guardianship.

The Book of Jubilees – Michael's Role as Guide and Advocate

The Book of Jubilees, an ancient Jewish text that expands upon the stories in Genesis and Exodus, offers another dimension of Michael's role in guiding humanity. Although Jubilees is not part of the canonical Hebrew Bible, it holds significance in Jewish and Christian apocryphal literature. Here, Michael is seen acting as a teacher and guide, particularly to the patriarchs, assisting them in understanding and aligning with divine laws.

Michael's Role as Guide in Jubilees

The Book of Jubilees paints Michael as a mentor who instructs Moses in the heavenly tablets, which contain the laws and ordained times of God. In this text, Michael becomes a custodian of divine knowledge, ensuring that humanity remains connected to sacred wisdom and aligned with divine will. His guidance provides both structure and spiritual support, reinforcing the cosmic order established by God.

In Jubilees, Michael's guidance reflects his commitment to justice and order, emphasizing his desire to bring clarity to those who seek divine understanding. This role as a teacher and advocate complements his protective nature, highlighting his responsibility not only to guard but also to enlighten.

Ritual of Guidance and Clarity Inspired by the Book of Jubilees

This ritual invites Michael's wisdom to illuminate a path forward, especially when seeking guidance in times of confusion or decision-making.

Purpose: To connect with Michael's guidance for clarity and alignment with divine wisdom.

Materials Needed:

- A blue or silver candle (representing clarity and divine wisdom)
- A journal and pen
- Myrrh incense (for invoking divine presence)
- A passage from the Book of Jubilees or a personal prayer seeking wisdom

Preparation: Begin by setting a serene space where you can focus and meditate without interruption. Place the candle and journal in front of you, lighting the incense to set a contemplative atmosphere.

Step-by-Step Instructions:

1. **Centering and Setting Intentions**
   Light the candle and take a few deep breaths, focusing on your intention to seek guidance. Imagine Michael's presence gently illuminating your mind, bringing clarity and insight.

   Say:
   "Saint Michael, bearer of divine wisdom, I seek your guidance. Show me the way forward and grant me the clarity to align my actions with divine truth."

2. **Reading or Reciting a Passage**
   If you have a passage from Jubilees, read it slowly,

letting the words inspire you. If not, say a personal prayer, asking Michael to open your mind to divine guidance and clarity.

3. **Journaling for Insight**
   With Michael's presence in mind, write down any thoughts, questions, or decisions weighing on you. Allow your thoughts to flow freely onto the page, letting Michael's energy bring clarity as you reflect.

   Prompt:
   "In the light of Saint Michael's wisdom, I seek understanding. What path brings me closest to divine truth?"

4. **Prayer for Continued Guidance**
   Place your hands over the journal, symbolizing your openness to ongoing guidance.

   Say:
   "Michael, guardian of wisdom, continue to guide me as I walk this path. May your presence be a lamp unto my feet, illuminating each step with clarity and purpose."

5. **Closing**
   Let the candle burn as you sit in quiet reflection, allowing any remaining thoughts or insights to surface. Extinguish the candle when you feel ready, preserving the journal entry for later review.

Post-Ritual Reflection
Over the next few days, revisit your journal entry to see if new insights arise. Michael's role as a teacher and guide often works gradually, revealing clarity over time. Trust in his wisdom and remain open to subtle signs or intuitions.

Integrating the Old Testament's Perspectives on Michael

The Old Testament and its apocryphal texts position Michael as both a fierce protector and a wise guide, offering a dual approach to understanding his influence. Reflecting on Daniel 12:1 and the Book of Jubilees allows practitioners to align with Michael's energy for both protection and guidance, reinforcing their faith in divine support through life's trials and decisions.

By embodying these teachings, practitioners can find strength in knowing they are not alone. Michael's guardianship and wisdom remain accessible through prayer, ritual, and meditative practice, allowing a deeper connection to divine justice and insight as conveyed in ancient texts.

New Testament Teachings Related to Michael: The Battle Against Darkness and the Mission of Angelic Guardianship

The New Testament provides powerful insights into the role of Saint Michael, specifically portraying him as a divine warrior and guardian in the apocalyptic struggle between good and evil. Through the Book of Revelation, Michael is introduced as the archangel leading the heavenly hosts against Satan, cementing his position as a protector of the divine order. Meanwhile, in the Book of Hebrews, angels are described as spiritual guardians tasked with serving humanity, which broadens our understanding of angelic roles and Michael's commitment to guiding and protecting souls. This section explores these New Testament perspectives, providing a foundation for spiritual practices that seek to align with Michael's strength, protection, and divine guardianship.

Revelation 12:7-9 – The Battle of Cosmic Proportions

The Book of Revelation brings forth a vivid depiction of Saint Michael in his role as the celestial warrior. Revelation 12:7-9 describes a great cosmic battle where Michael and his angels confront and ultimately vanquish Satan and his followers. This passage emphasizes Michael's role as the leader of the heavenly forces and the protector of divine order:

"Then war broke out in heaven. Michael and his angels fought against the dragon, and the dragon and his angels fought back. But he was not strong enough, and they lost their place in heaven. The great dragon was hurled down— that ancient serpent called the devil, or Satan, who leads the whole world astray. He was hurled to the earth, and his angels with him." (Revelation 12:7-9, NIV)

The Symbolism of Michael's Battle with the Dragon

This passage reveals Michael's profound role as the defender of heaven, casting out the forces that seek to disrupt divine harmony. The dragon, representing Satan, symbolizes the forces of chaos, deception, and rebellion against divine will. Michael, as the leader of the heavenly hosts, symbolizes divine justice, protection, and ultimate victory over darkness. His actions underscore the commitment to righteousness, aligning heaven's forces against the destructive influences of evil.

Michael's role in this battle serves as a reminder of the cosmic conflict between good and evil, an eternal struggle where each soul must choose alignment with divine or chaotic forces. For practitioners, Michael's victory over Satan becomes a source of courage, protection, and empowerment in their own spiritual battles against fear, doubt, and negativity.

Ritual of Spiritual Warfare: Invoking Michael's Protection and Strength

Drawing from Revelation 12:7-9, this ritual invites practitioners to connect with Michael's energy as a divine warrior, offering protection and strength against spiritual challenges or personal battles with negativity.

Purpose: To invoke Saint Michael's strength to guard against spiritual disturbances, negativity, or inner battles that require divine support.

Materials Needed:

- A red candle (symbolizing strength and protection)
- Frankincense incense (for purification and invoking angelic presence)
- A small sword or dagger, or an image of one, to represent Michael's weapon against darkness
- A printed or written copy of Revelation 12:7-9

Preparation: Begin by creating a quiet and focused space. Place the candle, incense, and sword (or image) on an altar or clean surface. Light the incense to begin clearing any negative energies from your space.

Step-by-Step Instructions:

1. **Centering and Invocation**
   Light the red candle, visualizing it as a beacon of Michael's protective energy. Close your eyes, taking several deep breaths, and imagine a sphere of radiant, red-tinged light surrounding you.

   Say:
   "Saint Michael, divine warrior and defender, I call upon you. Guide me through this struggle, shield me from harm, and lend me your strength to stand against all that seeks to undo me."

2. **Reading Revelation 12:7-9**
   Slowly read Revelation 12:7-9 aloud, allowing each word to resonate. As you read, envision Michael wielding his sword, casting out shadows and dispelling any negative forces.
3. **Symbolic Gesture with the Sword or Dagger**
   Take the sword or dagger (or place your hand over the image) and hold it up in front of you, imagining it charged with Michael's power. If comfortable, make a sweeping gesture as though clearing away darkness from your space.

   Say:
   "With the power of your sword, Michael, I banish all negativity and shadow. May no force of darkness disturb this sacred space."

4. **Prayer for Protection and Strength**
   With eyes closed, hold the sword or image over your heart, envisioning Michael's protective strength filling you with courage and resilience.

   Say:
   "Great Michael, who cast down the dragon, stand with me now. Protect me from fear, shield me from harm, and empower me to walk in the light. With you, I am safe, and with your strength, I am steadfast."

5. **Closing**
   Extinguish the candle when ready, and place the sword or dagger on your altar or somewhere meaningful to remind you of Michael's protection. Keep the printed verse close to reflect upon Michael's divine guardianship.

Post-Ritual Reflection
After performing this ritual, spend some time in quiet reflection. Consider how Michael's strength can be a source of courage in daily life. Reaffirm your alignment with divine

light, recognizing Michael as a powerful ally in your spiritual journey.

Hebrews 1:14 – The Ministry of Angelic Guardianship

The Book of Hebrews offers another perspective on angelic roles, referring to angels as "ministering spirits" assigned to guide and protect humanity. In Hebrews 1:14, angels are defined as beings who serve on behalf of those destined for salvation:

"Are not all angels ministering spirits sent to serve those who will inherit salvation?" (Hebrews 1:14, NIV)

Michael's Role as Guardian in Hebrews

While Hebrews does not explicitly mention Michael, this verse contextualizes the purpose of angelic beings as servants and protectors of humanity, especially those aligned with divine purpose. Within this framework, Michael's presence as a chief archangel becomes even more significant. His guardianship is not limited to defense in battle but also extends to the continual support and guidance of souls seeking spiritual truth. Michael's mission includes nurturing faith, strengthening resolve, and guiding those who face spiritual uncertainty or fear.

The concept of Michael as a ministering spirit underscores his compassionate and supportive nature, offering aid not only in physical or external struggles but also in the internal battles of faith, doubt, and alignment with the divine.

Ritual of Angelic Guardianship: Inviting Michael's Guidance and Protection

This ritual focuses on invoking Michael's presence as a guardian and guide, inviting him to walk alongside you in your spiritual journey and fortify your connection to divine support.

Purpose: To invite Michael's protective and guiding energy, enhancing one's spiritual resolve and opening oneself to divine wisdom.

Materials Needed:

- A white candle (representing purity and angelic guidance)
- Lavender or sandalwood incense (to promote peace and clarity)
- A feather or small white cloth, symbolizing angelic guardianship
- A copy of Hebrews 1:14 or a personally written prayer asking for guidance

Preparation: Begin by setting up a calm and peaceful space, placing the candle, incense, and feather (or cloth) in front of you. Light the incense and allow its calming scent to permeate your space, setting the tone for gentle reflection.

Step-by-Step Instructions:

1. **Setting the Intention for Guidance and Protection**
   Light the white candle, focusing on its soft glow as a symbol of Michael's calming, protective presence. Take a few deep breaths, letting go of tension and inviting a sense of openness.

   Say:
   "Saint Michael, beloved guardian and guide, I invite you to stand by my side. Walk with me on this path, protect me from harm, and lead me toward truth and wisdom."

2. **Reading Hebrews 1:14**
   Read Hebrews 1:14 aloud, embracing the concept of

angelic guardianship. Allow the words to inspire a sense of trust in the support available to you.

3. **Holding the Feather or Cloth**
Take the feather or cloth in your hands, holding it close to your heart. Envision it as a symbol of Michael's ever-present guardianship, a reminder that he walks with you through all experiences.

Say:
"With this symbol, I accept your protection and guidance, Saint Michael. Lead me forward with courage and light, that I may walk my path with faith."

4. **Prayer for Continued Support and Strength**
As you hold the feather or cloth, silently or aloud, offer a prayer for ongoing support and strength. Ask Michael to help you face each day with clarity and courage.

Say:
"Michael, ministering spirit and friend, I am grateful for your presence. Guide my steps, protect my heart, and strengthen my spirit. May I always walk in alignment with divine love."

5. **Closing**
Place the feather or cloth somewhere meaningful to remind you of Michael's protective guidance. Allow the candle to burn down or extinguish it as a sign of your continued trust in his guardianship.

Post-Ritual Reflection

In the days following the ritual, carry the feather or cloth with you, or place it near your bed as a reminder of Michael's presence. In moments of doubt or uncertainty, take a moment to hold the item and reaffirm your connection to his guidance, allowing his light to calm and strengthen you.

Integrating New Testament Teachings on Michael into Daily Life

Both Revelation and Hebrews provide complementary perspectives on Michael's role, showing him as both warrior and gentle guardian. Through Revelation, Michael's fierce strength offers protection against external and internal darkness. Hebrews, on the other hand, invites us to see Michael's guardianship as part of an ongoing spiritual journey, where divine guidance is a constant source of support.

By understanding Michael's role through these passages, practitioners can embrace his multifaceted presence—finding strength in times of trial, clarity in moments of uncertainty, and peace in the assurance of his protection. Engaging with these rituals and teachings, practitioners deepen their connection to Michael's divine energy, enhancing their spiritual resilience and alignment with the light.

Jewish Mystical Interpretations of Michael: Advocate and Celestial Guide

Jewish mystical texts provide rich insights into the role of Saint Michael, portraying him not only as a warrior but as a compassionate advocate and heavenly guide. In the Talmud and Zohar, Michael is depicted as a powerful intercessor for Israel, an angel who stands at the heart of celestial dynamics and aids humanity on its spiritual journey. Understanding these teachings allows us to access a more nuanced perception of Michael, whose energies are protective, compassionate, and supportive in spiritual growth. These mystical interpretations encourage a deeper engagement with Michael as an intercessor and a guide through life's spiritual challenges.

Talmudic Teachings on Michael as the Advocate of Israel

The Talmud, a central text of Rabbinic Judaism, frequently acknowledges Michael as an angel of advocacy, particularly for the people of Israel. As the protector and advocate of Israel, Michael's role is unique in the angelic hierarchy, bringing him close to human concerns and struggles. This role emphasizes Michael's compassionate nature, highlighting his capacity to plead for mercy and aid those in need. His advocacy is less about direct intervention and more about aligning the people with divine will, ensuring that they remain in harmony with spiritual laws.

The Talmud describes Michael's advocacy in various ways, such as interceding during times of judgment or standing as a "defender" when Israel's fate is questioned. Unlike other angels who serve specific roles without deviation, Michael's role is inherently dynamic, reflecting both his leadership and his compassionate nature. For practitioners, this Talmudic view offers a sense of comfort and connection, portraying Michael as an angel actively engaged in guiding and advocating for humanity, particularly in times of spiritual challenge.

Ritual for Invoking Michael's Advocacy

This ritual aims to connect practitioners with Michael's compassionate, protective energy, inviting him to act as an advocate during times of personal difficulty or self-doubt.

Purpose: To invoke Saint Michael as an advocate, seeking his intercession and support in moments of spiritual or emotional trial.

Materials Needed:

- A blue or white candle (symbolizing Michael's compassionate energy)

- A small bowl of water (representing purity and cleansing)
- Incense, such as frankincense or myrrh (for purification and angelic connection)
- A copy of a meaningful Talmudic verse or personal prayer asking for guidance and protection

Preparation: Arrange the candle, bowl of water, and incense on a table or altar. Create a quiet, reflective space, free from distractions.

Step-by-Step Instructions:

1. **Lighting the Candle and Incense**
   Light the blue or white candle to symbolize Michael's presence. Light the incense, allowing the smoke to cleanse the space and act as a medium for your invocation. Visualize the candle's light expanding around you, filling the space with a peaceful, protective energy.

   Say:
   "Saint Michael, advocate of compassion, I call upon your guidance. Stand with me in this moment of need, and help me find clarity and strength."

2. **Inviting Michael's Presence through Water Cleansing**
   Dip your fingers into the bowl of water, sprinkling it around you to symbolize purification. This water cleansing represents your openness to Michael's guidance and advocacy.

   Say:
   "With this water, I cleanse myself of fear and doubt. I welcome the presence of Saint Michael, my advocate and guide."

3. **Reading the Talmudic Passage or Personal Prayer**
   Read a passage from the Talmud or recite a personal

prayer that resonates with Michael's role as an advocate. Allow the words to settle within, reinforcing your trust in his guidance.

Example:
"Michael, protector and advocate, I ask for your intercession. As you stood for Israel, stand with me now. May your presence be my strength, your guidance my path."

4. **Visualization of Michael's Supportive Energy**
   Close your eyes and visualize Michael standing beside you, emanating a calm, compassionate energy. Imagine him holding a shield of light that wards off negativity, encouraging your spirit to rise with resilience.

   Say:
   "Saint Michael, be my advocate in times of trial. Let your light protect me, your strength uplift me, and your compassion fill my heart."

5. **Closing**
   Let the candle burn for a few minutes as you sit in silent reflection. When ready, extinguish the candle and thank Michael for his guidance.

Post-Ritual Reflection
After the ritual, write down any insights or feelings of peace that emerged. Reflect on how Michael's advocacy can be a source of strength in challenging times, reminding you that his compassion and guidance are always accessible.

Insights from the Zohar on Michael's Roles and Symbolism

The Zohar, a foundational work in Jewish mysticism, offers a profound perspective on Michael's role in the heavenly realms. Unlike the Talmud, which emphasizes his advocacy, the Zohar portrays Michael as an active force in divine dynamics. Here, Michael's essence is deeply connected with fire, representing purity, transformation, and divine judgment. He stands at the right hand of God, symbolizing mercy and benevolence. This association with fire and divine mercy highlights Michael's dual nature—he is both a protector and a purifier, wielding fire not for destruction but for transformation.

In the Zohar, Michael's fiery essence is linked to the south direction, symbolizing warmth, growth, and the expansive nature of divine love. Through this symbolism, the Zohar reveals a powerful insight: Michael's energy is a balancing force that brings spiritual warmth and purification, encouraging practitioners to embrace personal transformation. His fire is not one of punishment but of cleansing, inspiring a journey of inner purification aligned with divine will.

Ritual of Purification and Transformation with Michael's Fiery Essence

This ritual draws upon Michael's fiery energy as described in the Zohar, aiming to help practitioners release what no longer serves them and embrace a path of transformation.

Purpose: To connect with Michael's transformative, purifying energy, seeking release from negativity and a renewed sense of purpose.

Materials Needed:

- A red or white candle (symbolizing Michael's purifying fire)
- Cedar or sage incense (for purification)
- A small piece of paper and pen (for writing down aspects to release)
- A fire-safe bowl (to safely burn the paper)

Preparation: Set up the candle, incense, and fire-safe bowl in a safe, open space. Ensure there is no wind or flammable material nearby.

Step-by-Step Instructions:

1. **Lighting the Candle and Incense**
   Light the candle and incense, focusing on their flames and smoke as symbols of purification. Allow the candle's flame to represent Michael's fiery essence, bringing warmth and clarity.

   Say:
   "Saint Michael, bearer of divine fire, I invite your presence. Help me release what I no longer need and embrace transformation with an open heart."

2. **Writing Intentions for Release**
   On the piece of paper, write down any fears, habits, or feelings that you wish to release. Be honest, allowing this act of writing to be a commitment to transformation.

   Say:
   "With this, I offer all that holds me back. Michael, let your fire purify these burdens and transform them into light."

3. **Burning the Paper**
   Place the paper in the fire-safe bowl and carefully ignite it with the candle's flame. Watch as it burns, visualizing the energy of these thoughts or habits being released and transformed.

   Say:
   "As this burns, I am cleansed and renewed. Michael, with your fire, I am free of the old, open to the new."

4. **Visualization of Inner Light and Strength**
   Close your eyes, focusing on the warmth of the

candle's flame. Imagine Michael's light filling you from within, bringing clarity, strength, and a sense of peace. Allow this visualization to ground you in a renewed sense of purpose.

Say:
"Saint Michael, with your guidance, I am renewed. Let your light be my strength, your fire my guide, as I walk this path."

5. **Closing**
   Allow the candle to burn down as a symbol of ongoing transformation or extinguish it as you end the ritual. Sit for a few moments, embracing the peace and clarity brought by this act of purification.

Post-Ritual Reflection
In the days following, focus on the qualities you intend to embody after releasing negativity. Write about your experience in a journal, noting any shifts in thoughts or behaviors. Let Michael's transformative energy remind you that growth is a continual process, and that his fire is always available to purify and guide.

Embracing Michael's Mystical Roles in Daily Practice

The Talmud and Zohar collectively illuminate Michael as both an advocate and a purifier, revealing a unique duality in his essence. As a compassionate intercessor, he advocates for those in need, bringing solace and support to those facing challenges. In his Zoharic form, Michael's fiery energy catalyzes inner transformation, helping practitioners embrace growth and spiritual renewal. Together, these roles offer a holistic view of Michael's presence as an angel who both guards and transforms, providing a model for spiritual integrity and resilience.

By incorporating these teachings into ritual practices, practitioners engage deeply with Michael's energy, fostering a sense of inner strength, clarity, and alignment with divine purpose. Through reflection, ritual, and intention, one may continue to nurture a close relationship with Michael's guidance, creating a sacred foundation upon which to build a life of compassion, courage, and spiritual insight.

Apocryphal Accounts of Michael's Work: Pathways of Guidance and Spiritual Ascent

In the ancient apocryphal texts, Saint Michael emerges as more than a warrior; he is depicted as a profound guide, mentor, and gatekeeper of hidden realms, assisting souls in both spiritual ascent and repentance. The *Ascension of Isaiah* and *The Life of Adam and Eve* offer invaluable insights into Michael's role in leading souls through realms beyond the earthly and encouraging spiritual purification and reconciliation with the divine. These texts invite practitioners to seek deeper connections with Michael's guidance, exploring not only protection and strength but also the wisdom he provides on spiritual ascent and inner transformation.

The Ascension of Isaiah: Michael as a Guide to Hidden Realms

The *Ascension of Isaiah,* an early Christian apocryphal text, presents Saint Michael as an angelic guide who reveals hidden realms to the prophet Isaiah. In this narrative, Michael accompanies Isaiah through various celestial levels, where he encounters both angelic beings and divine light. Michael's guidance here represents his role as a mentor for those seeking spiritual knowledge, offering clarity and protection as they journey into unfamiliar spiritual territories. This guiding role is not merely about showing the way but about preparing and strengthening the soul to experience realms where divine presence is more pronounced, intense, and transformative.

This text highlights Michael's role in helping us understand that spiritual ascension involves more than gaining insight—it requires readiness, purification, and the courage to move beyond ordinary perception. Michael acts as a stabilizing force, ensuring that Isaiah can withstand the powerful revelations encountered in each realm. This guiding presence can similarly be invoked today, especially in meditation or ritual, as one seeks to access deeper layers of spiritual reality and connect with higher consciousness.

Ritual of Invocation for Spiritual Guidance and Exploration

This ritual invokes Michael's presence to guide the practitioner into deeper spiritual realms, echoing his role in *The Ascension of Isaiah*.

Purpose: To call upon Michael for guidance, protection, and preparation in exploring the higher spiritual realms, allowing the practitioner to encounter insights and divine truths safely.

Materials Needed:

- A white candle (symbolizing divine light and spiritual purity)
- A small bowl of saltwater (representing cleansing and preparation)
- Lavender or frankincense incense (to elevate spiritual awareness)
- A journal or notebook for reflections

Preparation: Arrange the candle, saltwater, and incense on a clean, sacred space. Light the candle to create a focal point of Michael's light. Begin with a few moments of centering breath, focusing on clearing your mind and heart.

Step-by-Step Instructions:

1. **Lighting the Incense and Candle**
   Light the incense, allowing its scent to fill the space as a marker of spiritual focus. As you light the candle, focus on its flame as a representation of Michael's guiding light.

   Say:
   "Saint Michael, guide of souls and revealer of mysteries, I invite your presence. Illuminate my path as you did for Isaiah, and help me to see with clarity and courage."

2. **Purification with Saltwater**
   Dip your fingers in the saltwater, anointing your forehead, and imagine Michael's energy clearing away any doubts or impurities. This step prepares you to approach hidden realms with purity and readiness.

   Say:
   "With this cleansing, I release all that does not serve me, opening myself to divine truth. Michael, may your light be my protection and your presence my strength."

3. **Guided Visualization of Ascending to the Higher Realms**
   Close your eyes and visualize a staircase of light ascending into the heavens. Picture Michael at your side, steadying and guiding you. With each step, feel yourself rising into realms of increasing clarity and light, seeing divine truths unfold around you. Imagine encountering insights relevant to your spiritual path, with Michael's presence allowing you to hold and understand these revelations.

   Say:
   "Saint Michael, I trust your guidance as I journey into realms unknown. Reveal to me what my soul seeks, and let your light illuminate all shadows."

4. **Silent Reflection and Connection**
   Spend a few moments in silence, absorbing any insights or feelings that arise. Trust that Michael's protection surrounds you as you open to new spiritual dimensions.
5. **Closing with Gratitude**
   When ready, visualize descending safely back to the earthly plane, accompanied by Michael's light. Open your eyes and extinguish the candle.

Say:
"Thank you, Saint Michael, for your guidance and protection. May your light remain with me as I carry these insights forward."

Post-Ritual Reflection
Journal about the experience, noting any messages, feelings, or visuals you encountered. Reflect on how these insights align with your spiritual path, seeking ways to apply them in daily life. Michael's guidance can help bring clarity to these reflections, showing how they connect to your purpose.

The Life of Adam and Eve: Michael's Teachings on Repentance and Spiritual Ascent

In *The Life of Adam and Eve*, an apocryphal text that narrates the lives of the first humans after their expulsion from Eden, Michael plays a central role in leading Adam and Eve toward repentance and reconciliation with the divine. Here, Michael embodies mercy and compassion, urging Adam and Eve to seek forgiveness and embark on a path of spiritual purification. This narrative illustrates Michael's support for the soul's journey of return to divine alignment, highlighting repentance as an essential aspect of spiritual ascent.

Michael's guidance in this text is multifaceted. He not only provides comfort to Adam and Eve but also directs them toward a disciplined path of atonement. This dual focus—comfort and discipline—mirrors Michael's capacity to support both the heart and the will, aligning the soul with divine purpose. By guiding practitioners in repentance, Michael invites them to release guilt and embrace spiritual growth, understanding that ascent often begins with humility and a desire to reconcile with the divine.

Ritual for Repentance and Spiritual Alignment

This ritual seeks to invoke Michael's guidance in personal repentance and spiritual alignment, echoing the teachings found in *The Life of Adam and Eve*.

Purpose: To call upon Michael for support in seeking forgiveness and guidance in moving forward on a path of spiritual integrity.

Materials Needed:

- A blue or purple candle (symbolizing mercy and repentance)
- A small piece of paper and pen (for writing personal intentions or confessions)
- A bowl of water (for symbolic cleansing)
- Sage or cedar incense (to clear negative energies)

Preparation: Arrange the candle, paper, water, and incense on a quiet surface, ideally in a space where you can sit comfortably in silence.

Step-by-Step Instructions:

1. **Lighting the Candle and Incense**
   Light the blue or purple candle and the incense, watching as the candle's flame grows steadily. Imagine

this flame as a source of Michael's compassionate guidance, reminding you of his supportive presence.

Say:
"Saint Michael, angel of mercy and guide of souls, I call upon you. Help me to release what burdens my spirit and align me with divine purpose."

2. **Writing Intentions of Repentance and Renewal**
   On the piece of paper, write down any thoughts, habits, or actions you wish to release, focusing on areas of your life where you feel misaligned. Be sincere, using this step as an opportunity to articulate your desire for spiritual growth.

   Say:
   "With these words, I acknowledge my journey and seek forgiveness. Michael, help me transform these burdens into opportunities for growth and alignment."

3. **Water Cleansing as Symbolic Release**
   Dip the paper in the bowl of water, allowing the ink to blur or dissipate as a symbolic release of these intentions. Visualize Michael's light cleansing these energies, purifying your spirit and strengthening your resolve.

   Say:
   "In this water, I release what no longer serves. Michael, wash away my burdens and renew my spirit with your guidance."

4. **Silent Meditation and Inner Listening**
   Spend a few moments in silence, listening for any intuitive insights or feelings that arise. Allow yourself to feel the peace of having released these burdens, envisioning Michael's energy supporting you as you move forward.

5. **Closing with Gratitude and Intention**
   When ready, extinguish the candle, symbolizing a new

beginning. Express gratitude to Michael for his presence and guidance.

Say:
"Thank you, Saint Michael, for your compassion and guidance. I walk forward renewed, aligned with purpose, and open to the divine."

Post-Ritual Reflection
Write down any reflections on how this release feels and consider setting intentions to act in alignment with the insights you received. Michael's guidance is not only about letting go but about moving forward with integrity. Use this time to identify new actions or practices that will help you remain true to your spiritual path.

Integrating Michael's Apocryphal Teachings into Daily Life

The apocryphal narratives of *The Ascension of Isaiah* and *The Life of Adam and Eve* reveal Saint Michael as a compassionate guide and mentor, assisting souls in navigating complex spiritual paths. By approaching Michael not only as a guardian but as an advocate for inner growth, practitioners can deepen their spiritual practice, aligning with his teachings on accessing higher realms and releasing spiritual burdens. These rituals serve as powerful methods for experiencing Michael's guidance directly, emphasizing spiritual courage, integrity, and a deepened sense of divine connection.

The teachings in these texts illustrate that Michael's guidance extends far beyond mere protection—he is a beacon of spiritual wisdom and compassion, helping souls transform, release, and ascend. By invoking his presence in daily practices, we are reminded that spiritual growth is not a solitary journey but one shared with divine forces dedicated to our ultimate alignment and peace. Through regular engagement, Michael's presence becomes a source of strength and clarity, reinforcing our commitment to the path of spiritual ascent.

Final Reflections: Integrating the Teachings of Saint Michael

In our exploration of the teachings and perspectives associated with Saint Michael, we have ventured through profound spiritual, metaphysical, and practical realms. From understanding the Divine Image in humanity and the cosmic principles of balance, justice, and interconnectedness, to delving into Saint Michael's guidance on protection, purification, and discernment, each topic has illuminated aspects of our inner and outer worlds. By engaging with these teachings, we are invited not only to understand these concepts on a mental level but also to integrate them deeply into our everyday lives, embodying the wisdom and strength that Saint Michael represents.

Lessons Learned: Insights from Each Stage

Throughout these teachings, we have learned about humanity's divine potential and the importance of free will in choosing paths that honor both the light and the shadow within us. Saint Michael's guidance on justice reframes it not as retribution but as restoration, urging us to seek ways of healing and balance in every circumstance. We also explored the unity of all creation and the rhythmic cycles of order and chaos, as well as the invisible, spiritual realms where Michael's protective and guiding presence is paramount. Through each of these layers, Saint Michael's teachings encourage us to approach life with a sense of humility, strength, and purpose.

The focus on metaphysical principles has reinforced that everything in existence is interconnected, highlighting the cause and effect inherent in our actions. This awareness teaches us to walk with intention, understanding that each thought, word, and deed resonates through the cosmos. Through Michael's teachings on protection and magic, we have received practical tools for shielding ourselves from negative forces, transforming our energy, discerning truth, and maintaining balance within and around us.

Embracing Saint Michael's Legacy

The essence of Saint Michael's teachings is an invitation to live with courage, integrity, and divine alignment. His presence calls us to honor our own divinity, recognize our interconnectedness, and act with compassion and clarity. Each practice and ritual associated with these teachings has served as a means of grounding these lofty ideals into actionable steps, making them accessible and transformative. By embracing Michael's legacy, we are empowered to move forward as guardians of light in our own lives, capable of facing challenges with resilience and wisdom.

Final Instructions for Integration

To bring these teachings into daily life, consider the following practices as ways to internalize and embody what has been learned:

1. **Morning Invocation of Protection and Purpose**
   Begin each day by invoking Michael's light, asking for guidance and protection. Visualize his presence with you as a shield, and set a clear intention for how you want to act in alignment with the teachings you have explored. This morning invocation can be as simple as closing your eyes and saying, "Saint Michael, be with me today. Guide my actions, protect my spirit, and help me to walk with integrity and courage."
2. **Midday Reflection on Unity and Interconnectedness**
   Take a moment during the day to reflect on the unity of all creation. Visualize yourself as part of a web of light connecting you with others, the Earth, and all living beings. This brief reflection fosters compassion

and encourages mindful actions that honor the interconnectedness of all life.
3. **Evening Purification and Release**
At the end of each day, take time to clear your mind and heart of any negativity, asking Saint Michael to purify your energy and release any burdens. You might use a small ritual, such as lighting a candle and saying, "Saint Michael, cleanse me of today's worries and missteps. Help me to release and renew, that I may rest in peace and rise with clarity."
4. **Weekly Practice of Self-Reflection**
Dedicate a day each week to journal about your thoughts, intentions, and actions, particularly how they align with the principles of justice, compassion, and truth. Reflect on any areas where you felt challenged or where you succeeded, and ask Saint Michael for continued guidance in areas of growth. This practice solidifies your understanding of cause and effect, bringing greater awareness to your choices.
5. **Monthly Ritual for Spiritual Fortification**
Conduct a simple ritual each month to fortify your spirit. Light a blue or white candle, representing Michael's light, and spend time in silent meditation, visualizing his presence filling you with strength, courage, and divine clarity. This ritual serves to realign you with your highest intentions, reinvigorating your spiritual commitment.

Walking Forward with Saint Michael's Light

As you carry these teachings forward, remember that growth is a journey, not a destination. Saint Michael's presence serves as a constant reminder that you are not alone; his guidance and strength are always available to those who seek it with an open heart. Allow his legacy to inspire you, acting as a source of courage when you face challenges and a beacon of clarity when the path ahead seems uncertain.

By choosing to engage with these teachings, you have aligned yourself with a powerful force of light and wisdom. Take pride in the steps you have taken and continue to deepen your practice, knowing that each day brings new opportunities to embody the principles of unity, justice, and divine truth. In this way, you become a vessel of Michael's teachings, contributing to the greater harmony and spiritual evolution of the world around you.

May the light of Saint Michael guide your path with courage, wisdom, and unwavering strength. As you journey forward, may you find peace in the balance of life's light and shadow, resilience in times of challenge, and joy in the beauty of each moment. May your heart remain open to the wisdom of these teachings, and may your spirit grow in unity with all that is sacred and eternal. Remember that every step you take with intention and love creates ripples of goodness and light that extend beyond what you can see.

May you walk in harmony, knowing you are protected, guided, and deeply connected to the divine. And may the blessings of Saint Michael be with you always, as you bring forth the light within yourself to bless the world. Go forth with faith, strength, and the knowledge that you are never alone on this sacred path.

APPENDIX

Master Ritual Structure

This master ritual structure incorporates elements designed to establish a powerful, protected ritual space aligned with Saint Michael's influence, enabling deep spiritual work and connection. By following these detailed steps, you'll establish a clear and sacred environment for each individual ritual.

Preparation and Altar Setup

Purpose of the Altar Layout
The central altar represents Saint Michael's heart of guidance, unity, and divine power. Each directional altar channels elemental forces and aspects of Saint Michael's influence to support balance, protection, and insight.

1. The Central Altar

The central altar is the focal point, symbolizing the presence and protection of Saint Michael.

- **Items Needed:**
    - An icon or statue of Saint Michael
    - White or blue candle (for divine light)
    - Bowl of salt water (for grounding and purification)
    - Anointing oil, such as frankincense or myrrh
    - Sacred scripture or a meaningful spiritual text
- **Instructions for Setup:**
    - Place Saint Michael's image or icon in the center of the altar.
    - Position the candle and bowl of salt water to the left and right of the icon.
    - Place anointing oil and scripture at the front.
    - **Explanation**: Each item is a symbolic link to Saint Michael's qualities—protection,

purification, and divine wisdom—anchoring your intentions with his guidance.

2. The Directional Altars

Each directional altar channels one of the four elements, corresponding with different energies associated with Saint Michael's attributes:

- **North (Earth)**: Stability and grounding
    - **Items**: Green candle, crystal, bowl of salt
    - **Symbolism**: Provides grounding energy and protection.
- **West (Water)**: Intuition and cleansing
    - **Items**: Blue candle, seashell, bowl of water
    - **Symbolism**: Opens pathways for emotional healing and clarity.
- **South (Fire)**: Courage and transformation
    - **Items**: Red candle, piece of charcoal, or incense
    - **Symbolism**: Embodies Saint Michael's purifying and transformative fire.
- **East (Air)**: Insight and wisdom
    - **Items**: Yellow candle, feather, incense
    - **Symbolism**: Draws in clarity, wisdom, and divine understanding.

Each altar reinforces the central theme by bringing in an aspect of nature and connecting it to spiritual energies, balancing all forces around you.

Opening the Protective Circle

The protective circle sets a boundary, safeguarding the ritual from unwanted energies.

1. **Begin Facing East**: Hold a lit candle or stick of incense.
2. **Walk Clockwise**: Move around the space, visualizing a radiant barrier of light.

3. **Invocation**: As you walk, say,
   "I cast this circle in the name of Saint Michael, that it may be a boundary of light, love, and divine protection."

Explanation: Moving clockwise generates positive energy, and invoking Saint Michael invites his guidance, sealing the circle with divine protection.

Performing the Lesser Banishing Ritual of the Pentagram (LBRP)

The Purpose of the LBRP

The LBRP serves to:

1. **Clear the Space of Negative Influences**: It acts as a "banishing" ritual, pushing out stagnant or negative energies.
2. **Establish a Protective Boundary**: It creates a shield around the practitioner.
3. **Align with Divine Forces**: By invoking divine names and symbols, the practitioner aligns themselves with higher spiritual forces.
4. **Center and Empower the Practitioner**: The ritual empowers the practitioner and establishes a clear, focused mind.

Step-by-Step Instructions for the LBRP

1. Preparation

Stand Facing East: In ceremonial magick, the East is associated with beginnings, inspiration, and the rising sun, making it an ideal starting point.

Physical Position: Stand with feet together and arms at your sides, relaxed and focused.

Take a Moment to Center Yourself: Take a few deep breaths and clear your mind. Visualize yourself bathed in a column of pure, white light.

2. The Kabbalistic Cross

The Kabbalistic Cross establishes a connection with divine light, centering and grounding you. This invocation of divine names surrounds you with protective energy and prepares you for the pentagram ritual.

1. **Touch Forehead**:
   - **Words**: "Ateh" (Thou art)
   - **Meaning**: You're invoking the divine presence within yourself.
   - **Visualization**: Imagine a radiant light descending into your forehead.
2. **Touch Chest**:
   - **Words**: "Malkuth" (Kingdom)
   - **Meaning**: This represents the physical world and the manifestation of divine presence.
   - **Visualization**: Feel the light move from your head to your chest, grounding in your heart.
3. **Touch Right Shoulder**:
   - **Words**: "Ve-Geburah" (and the Power)
   - **Meaning**: Geburah represents strength and discipline.
   - **Visualization**: Visualize the light extending from your chest to your right shoulder.
4. **Touch Left Shoulder**:
   - **Words**: "Ve-Gedulah" (and the Glory)
   - **Meaning**: Gedulah represents mercy and loving-kindness.
   - **Visualization**: Feel the light cross from your right to your left shoulder.

5. **Clasp Hands at Heart in Prayer Position**:
    - **Words**: "Le-Olam, Amen" (Forever, Amen)
    - **Meaning**: You seal this invocation of divine light within and around you.
    - **Visualization**: Visualize the light radiating out, creating a sphere of protection.

3. Drawing the Pentagrams

The pentagrams create energetic "doors" that push out negative influences in each cardinal direction.

1. **Face East**:
    - **Draw the Banishing Pentagram**:
        - Start at your left hip and move up to the top point of the pentagram, down to the right hip, up to the left shoulder, across to the right shoulder, and back down to the left hip.
    - **Visualize**: Imagine a blazing, blue-white light tracing the pentagram in the air.
    - **Words**: "YHVH" (Yod-Heh-Vav-Heh, the Tetragrammaton)
        - **Meaning**: This is the name of God in the Hebrew tradition, representing divine creation and authority.
    - **Physical Act**: Thrust your hand forward through the center of the pentagram, visualizing it blazing brighter.
2. **Move to the South**:
    - **Repeat Drawing the Pentagram**: Follow the same steps as above, visualizing the pentagram in blue-white flame.
    - **Words**: "Adonai" (Lord)
        - **Meaning**: Another name for God, calling upon divine mastery and protection.
3. **Move to the West**:

- **Repeat Drawing the Pentagram**: Draw the pentagram and visualize the flame.
- **Words**: "Eheieh" (I Am)
  - **Meaning**: This name emphasizes God's presence and existence beyond time and space.

4. **Move to the North**:
   - **Repeat Drawing the Pentagram**: Draw the pentagram and visualize the flame.
   - **Words**: "Agla" (Ateh Gibor Le-Olam Adonai, meaning "Thou art mighty forever, O Lord")
     - **Meaning**: This name affirms God's eternal strength and protection.
5. **Return to the East**: After completing the circle, end facing East.

Explanation: Drawing each pentagram pushes out and banishes negative energies, while invoking divine names seals each direction with protective light.

4. Invoking the Archangels

This step invites the protective presence of the four archangels to guard each direction. You will visualize each angel's presence as you invite them. You will see them, their energy, their element, or their light.

1. **Stretch Out Arms to Form a Cross**:
   - **Words**:
     - "Before me, Raphael" (Archangel of Air, East, Yellow)
     - "Behind me, Gabriel" (Archangel of Water, West, Blue or Orange)
     - "At my right hand, Michael" (Archangel of Fire, South, Red, Heat)
     - "At my left hand, Uriel" (Archangel of Earth, North, Green)

- "Above me, Metatron." Raise your head and hands upward with palms open to the sky. His light appears above you and penetrates the top of your head shooting through your perineum to the ground (Metatron, as the highest archangel and keeper of divine wisdom, Bright White Light)
- "Below me, Sandalphon." His light shoots up through the ground piercing your the perineum, out the top of your head and into outer-space (Sandalphon, as the archangel linked with earthly grounding and prayer, connects you to the Earth, Turquoise light)
  - **Meaning**: You align yourself with the archangels associated with each element and direction, surrounding yourself with divine guardianship. This invocation aligns you with a full, balanced energetic structure, enveloped by both heavenly wisdom and earthly grounding, enhancing the protective and spiritual aspects of the ritual.
2. **Say Aloud**: "For about me flames the pentagram, and within me shines the six-rayed star."
   - **Explanation**: The pentagram represents divine protection, while the six-rayed star represents your higher self or divine essence, aligning you with cosmic forces.

Visualization: See each archangel standing in their respective direction, filling the space with light and strength.

5. The Kabbalistic Cross (Repetition)

To close, repeat the Kabbalistic Cross to seal the ritual and ground your energy.

1. **Touch Forehead**: "Ateh"
2. **Touch Chest**: "Malkuth"
3. **Touch Right Shoulder**: "Ve-Geburah"

4. **Touch Left Shoulder**: "Ve-Gedulah"
5. **Clasp Hands at Heart**: "Le-Olam, Amen"

Explanation: Repeating the Kabbalistic Cross reaffirms your alignment with divine energies and seals the protective circle you've established.

The LBRP is a ritual of spiritual hygiene, clearing unwanted energies and aligning the practitioner with divine forces. By establishing a shield of protection and focusing the mind, the LBRP creates an ideal foundation for deeper spiritual and ritual work. Through the repeated actions, visualizations, and sacred words, the practitioner is reminded of their connection to the divine and fortified to undertake their path with clarity and strength.

Calling in the Four Directions with Archangels

This invocation brings in protective forces from each direction, drawing upon Saint Michael's guidance through each element.

1. **Face East** (Air): Light the East candle.
    - **Words**: "Guardians of the East, Archangel Raphael, bring clarity, insight, and divine truth. I invite your wisdom to join this sacred space."
2. **Face South** (Fire): Light the South candle.
    - **Words**: "Guardians of the South, Archangel Michael, bring courage, strength, and purification. I invite your transformative fire to join this sacred space."
3. **Face West** (Water): Light the West candle.
    - **Words**: "Guardians of the West, Archangel Gabriel, bring intuition, healing, and cleansing waters. I invite your soothing energy to join this sacred space."

4. **Face North** (Earth): Light the North candle.
    - **Words**: "Guardians of the North, Archangel Uriel, bring stability, grounding, and protection. I invite your enduring strength to join this sacred space."

Explanation: Invoking each direction brings specific, harmonizing energies. The archangels strengthen the protective circle, embodying virtues that enhance Saint Michael's guidance.

Grounding with the Middle Pillar Ritual

The Purpose of the Middle Pillar Ritual

The Middle Pillar Ritual is designed to:

1. **Channel Divine Light**: It brings spiritual energy from the higher planes into the body, allowing the practitioner to connect with divine wisdom.
2. **Balance and Ground the Practitioner**: Each energy center grounds different aspects of consciousness and promotes physical, emotional, and mental balance.
3. **Strengthen the Aura**: By filling each center with light, the ritual strengthens the aura, creating a powerful shield against external influences.

Step-by-Step Instructions for the Middle Pillar Ritual

1. Preparation and Centering

- **Stand Facing East**: Begin in a standing position with feet shoulder-width apart, hands relaxed at your sides, facing East.

- **Center Yourself**: Close your eyes, take several deep breaths, and focus on relaxing your body and calming your mind.

2. Visualize the Descent of Divine Light

- Imagine a brilliant sphere of white light descending from above, representing divine energy. This light enters through the crown of your head, initiating a flow of spiritual energy down through the body.

3. Kether: The Crown (Top of the Head)

1. **Visualize**: See a bright sphere of pure, white light forming at the crown of your head, about the size of a grapefruit.
2. **Vibrate**: Say aloud or vibrate the Hebrew word **"Ehyeh"** (pronounced Eh-HEH-yeh), meaning "I Am."
   - **Meaning**: Ehyeh, associated with Kether (the highest Sephirah on the Tree of Life), represents pure being and the source of divine consciousness.
3. **Visualization and Feeling**: Visualize the light at your crown pulsing and expanding with each vibration, filling your head with a sense of connection to divine wisdom.
4. **Physical Action**: If desired, you can gently place your hands over your crown to deepen focus on this center.

4. Da'at: The Throat (Throat Chakra)

1. **Visualize**: Allow the light to move down to the throat area, forming a smaller sphere of light.

2. **Vibrate**: Say **"YHVH Elohim"** (Yod-Heh-Vav-Heh El-oh-HEEM), meaning "Lord God."
   - **Meaning**: This divine name is associated with knowledge, communication, and clarity, and it brings divine understanding.
3. **Visualization and Feeling**: See the light glowing brightly in your throat, feeling a sense of divine truth and expression as the energy strengthens.
4. **Physical Action**: Place one or both hands near the throat to focus energy here.

5. Tiphareth: The Heart (Heart Chakra)

1. **Visualize**: See the light move further down into the center of your chest, forming a sphere of warm, golden light.
2. **Vibrate**: Say **"YHVH Eloah V'Daath"** (Yod-Heh-Vav-Heh El-oh-AH V'dah-AHT), meaning "Lord God of Knowledge."
   - **Meaning**: This divine name is associated with Tiphareth, symbolizing beauty, balance, and love.
3. **Visualization and Feeling**: Imagine this golden light filling your chest, radiating warmth, compassion, and equilibrium.
4. **Physical Action**: Place your hands over your heart, feeling the light expand with each breath, connecting with a sense of unity and harmony.

6. Yesod: The Genital Area (Sacral Center)

1. **Visualize**: Let the light move down to the pelvic area, forming a sphere of silvery-purple light.
2. **Vibrate**: Say **"Shaddai El Chai"** (Shah-DYE El-CHAI), meaning "Almighty Living God."

- **Meaning**: This name corresponds with Yesod, representing the foundation and the subconscious mind.
3. **Visualization and Feeling**: Visualize this light growing brighter, balancing and energizing the lower chakras and connecting you to vitality.
4. **Physical Action**: Place hands over this center if desired, feeling the stabilizing energy within your core.

7. Malkuth: The Feet (Grounding Center)

1. **Visualize**: Allow the light to flow down into your feet, forming a sphere of golden-green light at the soles of your feet.
2. **Vibrate**: Say **"Adonai ha-Aretz"** (Ah-do-NAI ha AH-retz), meaning "Lord of Earth."
   - **Meaning**: Malkuth represents the physical world and grounding.
3. **Visualization and Feeling**: Imagine roots of light extending from this sphere into the earth, grounding and connecting you with stability and strength.
4. **Physical Action**: Stand firmly and visualize the light anchoring deep into the earth, feeling balanced and secure.

8. Connecting the Spheres (Column of Light)

1. **Visualize a Column of Light**: Imagine a column of light running from Kether (the crown) down to Malkuth (the feet), connecting each sphere in a continuous line of energy.
2. **Vibration and Breathing**: As you breathe, visualize energy moving up and down this column, reinforcing the connection and balance between divine and earthly realms.

- Inhale as light flows up from your feet to your head, and exhale as it flows back down.
3. **Words to Say**: "May this light strengthen and align my spirit with divine purpose."

9. Close the Ritual with the Kabbalistic Cross

Repeat the Kabbalistic Cross to seal the energy, grounding the divine light within your body.

1. **Touch Forehead**: "Ateh"
2. **Touch Chest**: "Malkuth"
3. **Touch Right Shoulder**: "Ve-Geburah"
4. **Touch Left Shoulder**: "Ve-Gedulah"
5. **Clasp Hands at Heart**: "Le-Olam, Amen"

The Middle Pillar Ritual channels divine energy into your being, aligning your physical and spiritual centers with higher realms. This ritual enhances clarity, balance, and resilience, preparing you for deeper spiritual work.

Through each vibration, visualization, and physical gesture, the practitioner cultivates a powerful sense of centeredness, divine connection, and protection. Performing the Middle Pillar Ritual regularly strengthens the aura, provides grounding, and attunes the practitioner to a profound spiritual alignment, embodying the principles of the Kabbalistic Tree of Life.

Opening the Center Altar

This final opening step initiates the connection to Saint Michael directly.

1. **Light the Central Candle**: Approach the center altar and light the candle, symbolizing divine presence.
2. **Invocation**:
    - **Words**: "Saint Michael, Archangel of divine light and protection, I invite you into this sacred space. May your wisdom, courage, and strength fill this ritual and guide me."

Explanation: Lighting the central candle represents unity and the presence of Saint Michael. His qualities of protection and divine guidance are now fully invoked.

Performing the Specific Ritual

Follow the specific ritual steps as described for your chosen purpose (protection, purification, etc.). Each ritual integrates into the master structure but emphasizes a unique quality associated with Saint Michael.

Closing the Altars and Disposing of Remnants

Once the main ritual is complete, close the altars with gratitude and respect, symbolizing the return of energies to their natural balance.

1. **Closing Each Directional Altar**:
    - Begin in the North, moving counterclockwise.
    - Extinguish the North candle, saying, "Thank you, Arch Angel Uriel, Guardians of the North, for your grounding and strength. Depart in peace."
    - Continue to each direction, releasing the energies in gratitude. (East: Raphael and Guardians of the East; South: Michael and Guardians of the South; West: Gabriel and Guardians of the West)
2. **Closing the Central Altar**:
    - Extinguish the central candle.

- **Words**: "Saint Michael, I release you with gratitude and love. Thank you for your guidance and protection."
3. **Disposal of Remnants**: Respectfully return any ashes, salt, or water used in the ritual to nature by burying or pouring into running water.

Words for Disposing of Remnants

At a natural setting (running water, the earth, or a chosen disposal site):

Ashes: "As these ashes return to the earth, so too does the energy return to the cycles of life. I release you with respect and gratitude, honoring the transformation you have symbolized."

Salt or Water: "I return this salt (or water) to the earth, in gratitude and peace. May it carry with it all blessings and intentions, returned now to the flow of life."

Other Natural Remnants (such as herbs or flowers): "In the name of Saint Michael, I release these remnants. May they enrich the earth as symbols of wisdom, strength, and peace."

Accompanying Gesture:

As you speak these words, sprinkle the remnants into running water, scatter them over the earth, or bury them gently. Place your hand over your heart, then extend it outward as a gesture of release and gratitude.

Final Words: "Thank you, Saint Michael and the Divine Archangels, for your presence, guidance, and protection. May the energy of this ritual harmonize with creation and return in peace. The work is complete."

Explanation: Disposing of remnants with care honors the sacred energies that were invoked and completes the cycle, closing the ritual with respect.

Final Words of Integration

After closing, take a moment for reflection and grounding.

1. **Grounding Visualization**: Envision roots extending from your feet into the earth, connecting with Saint Michael's enduring strength.
2. **Words of Integration**:
    - "Saint Michael, may the lessons of this ritual remain with me, guiding my steps and strengthening my spirit. I walk with courage, faith, and an open heart."

Through this comprehensive ritual structure, you align with Saint Michael's protective and guiding energies, ready to carry these sacred lessons forward in daily life.

Step-by-Step Instructions for Creating Consecration Oil

Preparation

1. **Materials Needed**:
   - Small bottle or vial for the consecrated oil.
   - High-quality olive oil (traditionally used for consecration).
   - Optional essential oils (such as frankincense or myrrh for added spiritual symbolism).
   - White candle and matches or lighter.
   - Bible or a printout of selected scriptures (Psalm 23, John 14:27, or James 5:14-15).
   - Small bowl for mixing the oil, if needed.
   - Clean cloth or covering for the oil.
2. **Sacred Space**:
   - Find a quiet, clean place to conduct the ritual, free from distractions.
   - Set up a small altar if possible, placing a crucifix, image of the Virgin Mary, or Saint Michael (optional), along with the Bible, candle, and the oil bottle.

The Ritual

1. **Light the Candle**:
   - Light the white candle, representing the Holy Spirit's presence, purity, and divine light.
   - **Say**: "Lord, let your light guide this ritual. May your spirit of holiness be present as I prepare this oil for sacred purposes."
2. **Centering Prayer**:
   - Begin with a simple prayer to focus your mind and heart on God's presence.
   - **Say**: "Heavenly Father, I come before you with reverence and humility, asking for your blessing

upon this oil. May it serve as a vessel for your grace, your love, and your protection."

3. **Scripture Reading**:
   - Choose one or more scriptures to read aloud, inviting divine purpose into the ritual:
     - **Psalm 23:5**: "You anoint my head with oil; my cup overflows."
     - **John 14:27**: "Peace I leave with you; my peace I give to you. Not as the world gives do I give to you."
     - **James 5:14-15**: "Is anyone among you sick? Let them call the elders of the church to pray over them and anoint them with oil in the name of the Lord."

4. **Blessing the Oil**:
   - Pour the olive oil into the bowl or directly into the small vial.
   - Hold your hands over the oil and ask God's blessing upon it.
   - **Say**: "Lord, I ask you to bless this oil, that it may be a sign of your healing power, a vessel of your Holy Spirit, and a source of strength, peace, and blessing. May it bring comfort to those who use it and be consecrated for your service."

5. **Adding Essential Oils (Optional)**:
   - If you wish to add essential oils like frankincense (symbolizing divinity) or myrrh (symbolizing sacrifice and healing), add a drop or two now.
   - **Say**: "With these scents of frankincense and myrrh, I remember the gifts brought to our Savior, Jesus Christ. May this oil carry the same reverence and honor to those it anoints."

6. **Consecration of the Oil**:
   - Make the sign of the cross over the oil three times, as a symbol of consecration.
   - **Say**: "In the name of the Father, and of the Son, and of the Holy Spirit, I consecrate this oil. May it carry your presence, Lord, to heal, protect, and sanctify all who receive it."

7. **Final Prayer and Dedication**:

- Hold the oil container close to your heart or place your hands over it as a final blessing.
- **Say**: "Lord Jesus Christ, through the intercession of the Blessed Virgin Mary and Saint Michael the Archangel, I dedicate this oil to your service. Let it be a blessing to all who use it, a sign of your love, and an instrument of your peace. Amen."

8. **Sealing and Storing the Oil**:
    - Seal the bottle tightly.
    - Cover the container with a clean cloth to symbolize its sacredness, or place it on your altar if it will be used shortly.
    - If the oil will be stored, keep it in a clean, safe place, ideally in a place dedicated to prayer or reflection.

9. **Extinguishing the Candle**:
    - Close the ritual by extinguishing the candle, symbolizing the completion of the sacred act.
    - **Say**: "Thank you, Lord, for your blessing and presence in this holy work. May this oil carry your light and grace wherever it is needed. Amen."

Explanation of Each Step

- **Lighting the Candle**: Represents the Holy Spirit's light and sets a sacred tone.
- **Centering Prayer**: Grounds you in reverence, inviting humility and focus.
- **Scripture Reading**: Connects the act to biblical tradition, framing it in divine purpose.
- **Blessing and Consecrating the Oil**: Directly asks for God's blessing, dedicating the oil as a spiritual tool.
- **Optional Essential Oils**: Adds symbolic meaning, enhancing the ritual with scents used in biblical tradition.
- **Final Prayer**: Dedicates the oil completely to God, inviting Jesus' presence.

- **Sealing and Storing**: Safeguards the oil's purity, keeping it in a respectful place.
- **Extinguishing the Candle**: Concludes the ritual, affirming the sanctity of the consecration.

Using the Consecrated Oil

- When using the oil for anointing, you may say: "In the name of the Father, and of the Son, and of the Holy Spirit, may this oil bring you God's peace, protection, and healing. Amen."
- For blessing a space: Dab a small amount on windows or doorways, saying, "May this home be blessed, protected, and filled with God's light."

Step-by-Step Instructions for Creating Holy Water

Preparation

1. **Materials Needed**:
    - Clean, fresh water (preferably spring or distilled water).
    - Small bowl or glass container for holding the water.
    - A small vial or bottle for storing the holy water.
    - Optional salt (blessed if possible).
    - White candle and matches or lighter.
    - Bible or a printed scripture passage for blessing (John 4:14 or Psalm 51:7).
    - Cross or crucifix (optional but encouraged).
2. **Sacred Space**:
    - Find a quiet, clean space free from distractions where you can focus on the ritual.
    - Set up a small altar, if possible, with a crucifix, Bible, candle, and the water in its container.

The Ritual

1. **Lighting the Candle**:
    - Light the white candle to symbolize the presence of the Holy Spirit.
    - **Say**: "Lord, let your light and purity fill this space as I prepare this water for holy use."
2. **Centering Prayer**:
    - Begin with a prayer to focus your mind and heart on God's presence.
    - **Say**: "Heavenly Father, I ask that you bless this water, filling it with your love, peace, and power. May it serve as a sign of your presence and protection."
3. **Scripture Reading**:

- Read one or both of these scriptures to invite God's blessing upon the water:
  - **John 4:14**: "But whoever drinks the water I give them will never thirst. Indeed, the water I give them will become in them a spring of water welling up to eternal life."
  - **Psalm 51:7**: "Cleanse me with hyssop, and I will be clean; wash me, and I will be whiter than snow."

4. **Blessing and Exorcism of Salt (Optional)**:
   - If using salt, bless it as part of the ritual. Traditionally, salt is seen as a purifier and preserver.
   - **Words to Say**: "Almighty God, bless this salt. May it be a sign of your protection and purification, preserving us from all evil. In the name of the Father, the Son, and the Holy Spirit. Amen."
   - Add a pinch of salt to the water, stirring gently as a symbol of purity.

5. **Blessing the Water**:
   - Dip your fingers into the water, making the sign of the cross over it.
   - **Words to Say**: "Lord, by the power of your Holy Spirit, I ask you to bless this water. May it be a tool of healing, protection, and purification. May it carry your grace and presence wherever it flows."

6. **Invoking the Holy Spirit**:
   - Place your hands over the water, visualizing the presence of the Holy Spirit filling it with light.
   - **Say**: "Holy Spirit, descend upon this water. Consecrate it as a holy blessing for all who use it. May it bring peace, cleansing, and protection, in the name of the Father, and of the Son, and of the Holy Spirit. Amen."

7. **Making the Sign of the Cross Over the Water**:
   - With your hand, make the sign of the cross above the water three times to seal the blessing.

- **Words to Say**: "In the name of the Father, and of the Son, and of the Holy Spirit, I consecrate this water as holy, set apart for God's purpose."
8. **Final Dedication**:
    - Dedicate the water to God's service, praying it brings grace and protection to all it touches.
    - **Say**: "Lord Jesus Christ, may this water be a blessing to all who use it. Let it serve as a sign of your love and your power over all things. Amen."

Explanation of Each Step

- **Lighting the Candle**: Symbolizes God's presence, setting a sacred atmosphere.
- **Centering Prayer**: Focuses your intentions, inviting God to work through the water.
- **Scripture Reading**: Connects the ritual to biblical tradition, blessing the water with God's word.
- **Blessing and Exorcism of Salt**: Salt is used as a symbol of purity and protection, traditionally blessed to enhance the water's holy properties.
- **Blessing the Water**: Directly invites God's presence into the water, dedicating it as a sacred object.
- **Invoking the Holy Spirit**: Calls on the Holy Spirit to empower the water, infusing it with divine energy.
- **Making the Sign of the Cross**: Represents the Trinity, sealing the blessing in the water.
- **Final Dedication**: Dedicates the water for God's work, blessing all who come into contact with it.

Using the Holy Water

- **For Blessing Spaces**: Dip your fingers in the water, sprinkle it around the space, and say, "In the name of the Father, and of the Son, and of the Holy Spirit, may this space be blessed and protected."
- **For Personal Blessing**: Dip your fingers in the holy water, make the sign of the cross on your forehead,

and say, "In the name of the Father, and of the Son, and of the Holy Spirit. Amen."
- **For Anointing Objects**: Dip a finger in the holy water, trace the sign of the cross on the object, and say, "May this (object) be blessed for God's service and protection."

This Catholic-inspired ritual to create holy water is a reverent way to invite divine presence into an ordinary element, making it sacred and purposeful.

SOURCES

1. Human Nature

- **Bible (New Revised Standard Version or King James Version)**
    - Genesis 1:27
    - Deuteronomy 30:19-20
    - Psalm 139:23-24
- **The Midrash Tanhuma**
    - A collection of Jewish homiletic teachings on the Torah. See:
    - Bialik, Hayim Nahman, and Yehoshua Hana Rawnitzki. *The Book of Legends: Sefer Ha-Aggadah.* Schocken Books, 1992. ISBN 978-0805241136.
- **Apocrypha: The Life of Adam and Eve**
    - This text offers insights into human agency and sin. See:
    - Anderson, Gary A., and Michael E. Stone. *A Synopsis of the Books of Adam and Eve.* Brill, 1999. ISBN 978-9004116009.
- **The Wisdom of Solomon**
    - A deuterocanonical book, included in the Septuagint, that discusses wisdom and justice. See:
    - Harrington, Daniel J. *Invitation to the Apocrypha.* Eerdmans Publishing, 1999. ISBN 978-0802846334.

2. Divine Justice

- **Bible**
    - Isaiah 1:17
    - Micah 6:8
    - Galatians 6:7
- **Talmud, Berakhot**

- This section of the Talmud explores principles of justice and mercy. English translations are widely available; see:
- Neusner, Jacob. *The Talmud of Babylonia: An American Translation, Vol. 2 - Berakhot.* University of South Florida Press, 1991. ISBN 978-0891308549.
- **The Ascension of Isaiah**
  - An apocryphal text detailing Michael's roles as protector and guide.
  - Charles, R.H. *The Ascension of Isaiah.* Adamant Media Corporation, 2001. ISBN 978-1421252021.

3. Cosmic Truths

- **Bible**
  - Colossians 1:16-17
  - John 1:5
  - Ecclesiastes 3:1-8
- **The Zohar**
  - The foundational text of Kabbalistic thought, discussing cosmic order and unity.
  - Scholem, Gershom. *Zohar: The Book of Splendor.* Schocken Books, 1995. ISBN 978-0805210347.
- **Sefer Yetzirah (Book of Creation)**
  - An ancient text exploring cosmology, Hebrew letters, and creation.
  - Kaplan, Aryeh. *Sefer Yetzirah: The Book of Creation in Theory and Practice.* Weiser Books, 1997. ISBN 978-0877288558.

4. Hidden Realms

- **Bible**
  - Daniel 10:13
  - Ephesians 6:12
  - Matthew 7:7
- **Kabbalah and Merkabah Mysticism**

- o Discusses Jewish mystical traditions and realms.
- o Scholem, Gershom. *Major Trends in Jewish Mysticism*. Schocken Books, 1995. ISBN 978-0805210446.
- **The Book of Enoch**
  - o This apocryphal text explores angelic beings and realms.
  - o Knibb, Michael A. *The Ethiopic Book of Enoch*. Oxford University Press, 1978. ISBN 978-0198261632.

5. Metaphysical Principles Governing the Universe

- **Bible**
  - o Proverbs 11:1
  - o Job 4:8
  - o 1 Corinthians 12:12-27
- **Pirkei Avot (Ethics of the Fathers)**
  - o A foundational Jewish text on ethics, exploring balance and cause-effect.
  - o Telushkin, Joseph. *Jewish Wisdom: Ethical, Spiritual, and Historical Lessons from the Great Works and Thinkers*. William Morrow, 1995. ISBN 978-0688129581.
- **The Zohar**
  - o A Kabbalistic text exploring the interdependence of all beings.
  - o Berg, Michael. *The Essential Zohar: The Source of Kabbalistic Wisdom*. Harmony, 2004. ISBN 978-0609609865.

6. Magic from Saint Michael's Perspective

- **Bible**
  - o Psalm 91
  - o Isaiah 6:6-7
  - o John 8:32
  - o Matthew 12:43-45

- Psalm 104:4
- Exodus 30:25-29
- **Jewish Protective Prayers and Magic**
  - Trachtenberg, Joshua. *Jewish Magic and Superstition: A Study in Folk Religion.* University of Pennsylvania Press, 2004. ISBN 978-0812218626.
- **Kabbalah and the Magic of Fire Element**
  - Greer, John Michael. *The Element Encyclopedia of Secret Societies: The Ultimate A-Z of Ancient Mysteries, Lost Civilizations and Forgotten Wisdom.* HarperElement, 2006. ISBN 978-0007220683.
- **The Lesser Key of Solomon**
  - A classic grimoire containing protective and banishing spells; Michael is often invoked.
  - Peterson, Joseph H. *The Lesser Key of Solomon: Lemegeton Clavicula Salomonis.* Weiser Books, 2001. ISBN 978-1578632206.
- **Archangels and Angelic Magic**
  - Kaplan, Aryeh. *Meditation and Kabbalah.* Samuel Weiser, 1985. ISBN 978-0877286165.

7. Scriptural and Interpretative References on Michael

- **The Bible**
  - Daniel 12:1; Revelation 12:7-9; Hebrews 1:14
  - Use reputable study Bibles for historical and theological notes, such as the *HarperCollins Study Bible* (NRSV).
- **Deuterocanonical and Apocryphal Texts on Michael**
  - Charles, R.H. *The Apocrypha and Pseudepigrapha of the Old Testament, Volume II: Pseudepigrapha.* Clarendon Press, 1913. ISBN 978-0198261694.
- **The Zohar on Archangels**
  - The *Zohar* contains many references to the roles of archangels. See:

- o Matt, Daniel C. *The Zohar: Pritzker Edition, Volumes 1-12*. Stanford University Press, 2004-2017. ISBN 978-0804747479.
- **Talmudic Teachings on Michael**
  - o Jewish insights from the Talmud on Michael's protective roles. See:
  - o Steinsaltz, Adin. *The Talmud: A Reference Guide*. Random House, 1989. ISBN 978-0679405802.
- **Ascension of Isaiah and the Life of Adam and Eve**
  - o Charlesworth, James H. *The Old Testament Pseudepigrapha, Volume 2: Expansions of the "Old Testament" and Legends, Wisdom and Philosophical Literature, Prayers, Psalms, and Odes*. Yale University Press, 1985. ISBN 978-0300140194.

www.ingramcontent.com/pod-product-compliance
Lightning Source LLC
Chambersburg PA
CBHW070840160426
43192CB00012B/2260